Tehillim

Book of Psalms

King David

Jewish Edition

from
Hebrew Bible

SimchatChaim.com

There is no known book without mistakes. Therefore, I ask in every language of application if anyone has any questions, comments, clarifications, corrections, please send to: book@yahoo.com

All material used in this section may not be used for commercial purposes, but only for study and teaching.

To get this book or books and information Email me at:

book@yahoo.com

Copyright©All Rights Reserved to

www.simchatchaim.com

Itzhak Hoki Aboudi ©All rights reserved to the Editor

Second edition 2024

Tehillim- Book of Psalms

Tehillim - Book of Psalms

Tehillim - Book of Psalms, the first book of the section in the Hebrew Bible called Writings, is an anthology of 150 poems attributed to King David and to others. It includes songs of praise to God, laments of communal or personal tragedy, and expressions of anger, despair, hope, and gratitude. Psalms are prevalent throughout Jewish liturgy and commonly recited as an independent form of prayer. They are often sung or chanted.

In the Jewish tradition, the book is mainly attributed to King David and other personalities, but a number of psalms are dated in biblical studies to the time of the destruction of the First Temple and the days of the Second Temple. In the Jewish canon there are 150 chapters in the Book of Psalms.

The book is divided into five books like the five Pentacles of the Torah.
And these are:

Book 1 - Psalms 1–41
Book 2 - Psalms 42–72
Book 3 - Psalms 73–89
Book 4 - Psalms 90–106
Book 5 - Psalms 107–150

The Talmud comments: This opinion disputes that of Rabbi Yehoshua ben Levi, as Rabbi Yehoshua ben

Tehillim- Book of Psalms

Levi said: What is the meaning of the word halleluya? It means praise Him [halleluhu] with many praises [hillulim]. According to this opinion, the ya at the end of the word is a superlative, not a divine name.

The Talmud adds: This statement of Rabbi Yehoshua ben Levi disagrees with another ruling that he himself issued, as Rabbi Yehoshua ben Levi said: The book of Psalms is said by means of ten expressions of praise: By nitzuaḥ, niggun, maskil, mizmor, shir, ashrei, tehilla, tefilla, hoda'a, and halleluya. He continues: The greatest of them all is halleluya, as it includes God's name and praise at one time. This statement indicates that Rabbi Yehoshua ben Levi considers halleluya to be a combination of two words, one of which is the name of God.

Rav Yehuda said that Shmuel said: The song in the Torah, i.e., the Song at the Sea (Exodus 15:1–19), Moses and the Jewish people recited it when they ascended from the sea. The Talmud asks: And who said this hallel mentioned in the mishna, Psalms 113–118? The Talmud answers: The Prophets among them established this hallel for the Jewish people, that they should recite it on every appropriate occasion; and for every trouble, may it not come upon them, they recite the supplications included in hallel. When they are redeemed, they recite it over their redemption, as hallel includes expressions of gratitude for the redemption.

Tehillim- Book of Psalms

It was taught in a baraita that Rabbi Meir would say: All the praises stated in the book of Psalms were recited by David, as it is stated: "The prayers of David, son of Yishai, are ended [kalu]" (Psalms 72:20). Do not read kalu; rather, read kol elu, all of these, which indicates that the entire book of Psalms consists of the prayers of King David.

Tehillim- Book of Psalms

Tehillim- Book of Psalms

Tehillim - Book of Psalms

Chapter 1

HAPPY IS the man that hath not walked in the counsel of the wicked, nor stood in the way of sinners, nor sat in the seat of the scornful.

But his delight is in the law of the LORD; and in His law doth he meditates day and night.

And he shall be like a tree planted by streams of water, that bringeth forth its fruit in its season, and whose leaf doth not wither; and in whatsoever he doeth he shall prosper.

Not so the wicked; but they are like the chaff which the wind driveth away.

Therefore, the wicked shall not stand in the judgment, nor sinners in the congregation of the righteous.

For the LORD regardeth the way of the righteous; but the way of the wicked shall perish.

Chapter 2

Why are the nations in an uproar? And why do the peoples mutter in vain?

The kings of the earth stand up, And the rulers take counsel together, Against the LORD, and against His anointed:

Tehillim- Book of Psalms

'Let us break their bands asunder, and cast away their cords from us.'
He that sitteth in heaven laugheth, the Lord hath them in derision.
Then will He speak unto them in His wrath, and affright them in His sore displeasure:
'Truly it is I that have established My king upon Zion, My holy mountain.'
I will tell of the decree: The LORD said unto me: 'Thou art My son, this day have I begotten thee.
Ask of Me, and I will give the nations for thine inheritance, and the ends of the earth for thy possession.
Thou shalt break them with a rod of iron; Thou shalt dash them in pieces like a potter's vessel.'
Now therefore, O ye kings, be wise; be admonished, ye judges of the earth.
Serve the LORD with fear, and rejoice with trembling.
Do homage in purity, lest He be angry, and ye perish in the way, when suddenly His wrath is kindled. Happy are all they that take refuge in Him.

Chapter 3

A Psalm of David, when he fled from Absalom his son.
LORD, how many are mine adversaries become! Many are they that rise up against me.
Many there are that say of my soul: 'There is no salvation for him in God.' Selah

Tehillim- Book of Psalms

But thou, O LORD, art a shield about me; My glory, and the lifter up of my head.

With my voice I call unto the LORD, and He answereth me out of His holy mountain. Selah

I lay me down, and I sleep; I awake, for the LORD sustaineth me.

I am not afraid of ten thousands of people, that have set themselves against me round about.

Arise, O LORD; save me, O my God; for Thou hast smitten all mine enemies upon the cheek, Thou hast broken the teeth of the wicked.

Salvation belongeth unto the LORD; Thy blessing be upon Thy people. Selah

Chapter 4

For the Leader; with string-music. A Psalm of David.

Answer me when I call, O God of my righteousness, Thou who didst set me free when I was in distress; be gracious unto me, and hear my prayer.

O ye sons of men, how long shall my glory be put to shame, in that ye love vanity, and seek after falsehood? Selah

But know that the LORD hath set apart the godly man as His own; The LORD will hear when I call unto Him.

Tremble, and sin not; commune with your own heart upon your bed, and be still. Selah

Tehillim- Book of Psalms

Offer the sacrifices of righteousness, and put your trust in the LORD.

Many there are that say: 'Oh that we could see some good!' LORD, lift Thou up the light of Thy countenance upon us.

Thou hast put gladness in my heart, more than when their corn and their wine increase.

In peace will I both lay me down and sleep; for Thou, LORD, makest me dwell alone in safety.

Chapter 5

For the Leader; upon the Nehiloth. A Psalm of David.

Give ear to my words, O LORD, consider my meditation.

Hearken unto the voice of my cry, my King, and my God; For unto Thee do I pray.

O LORD, in the morning shalt Thou hear my voice; In the morning will I order my prayer unto Thee, and will look forward.

For Thou art not a God that hath pleasure in wickedness; Evil shall not sojourn with Thee.

The boasters shall not stand in Thy sight; Thou hatest all workers of iniquity.

Thou destroyest them that speak falsehood; The LORD abhorreth the man of blood and of deceit.

But as for me, in the abundance of Thy lovingkindness will I come into Thy house; I will bow down toward Thy holy temple in the fear of Thee.

Tehillim- Book of Psalms

O LORD, lead me in Thy righteousness because of them that lie in wait for me; Make Thy way straight before my face.

For there is no sincerity in their mouth; Their inward part is a yawning gulf, Their throat is an open sepulchre; They make smooth their tongue.

Hold them guilty, O God, Let them fall by their own counsels; Cast them down in the multitude of their transgressions; For they have rebelled against Thee.

So shall all those that take refuge in Thee rejoice, They shall ever shout for joy, And Thou shalt shelter them; Let them also that love Thy name exult in Thee.

For Thou dost bless the righteous; O LORD, Thou dost encompass him with favour as with a shield.

Chapter 6

For the Leader; with string-music; on the Sheminith. A Psalm of David.

O LORD, rebuke me not in Thine anger, Neither chasten me in Thy wrath.

Be gracious unto me, O LORD, for I languish away; Heal me, O LORD, for my bones are affrighted.

My soul also is sore affrighted; And Thou, O LORD, how long?

Return, O LORD, deliver my soul; Save me for Thy mercy's sake.

Tehillim- Book of Psalms

For in death there is no remembrance of Thee; In the nether-world who will give Thee thanks?

I am weary with my groaning; Every night make I my bed to swim; I melt away my couch with my tears.

Mine eye is dimmed because of vexation; It waxeth old because of all mine adversaries.

Depart from me, all ye workers of iniquity; For the LORD hath heard the voice of my weeping.

The LORD hath heard my supplication; The LORD received my prayer.

All mine enemies shall be ashamed and sore affrighted; They shall turn back; they shall be ashamed suddenly.

Chapter 7

Shiggaion of David, which he sang unto the LORD, concerning Cush a Benjamite.

O LORD my God, in Thee have I taken refuge; Save me from all them that pursue me, and deliver me;

Lest he tear my soul like a lion, rending it in pieces, while there is none to deliver.

O LORD my God, if I have done this; If there be iniquity in my hands;

If I have requited him that did evil unto me, Or spoiled mine adversary unto emptiness;

Let the enemy pursue my soul, and overtake it, And tread my life down to the earth; Yea, let him lay my glory in the dust. Selah

Tehillim- Book of Psalms

Arise, O LORD, in Thine anger, Lift up Thyself in indignation against mine adversaries; Yea, awake for me at the judgment which Thou hast commanded.
And let the congregation of the peoples compass Thee about, And over them return Thou on high.
O LORD, who ministerest judgment to the peoples, Judge me, O LORD, According to my righteousness, and according to mine integrity that is in me.
Oh that a full measure of evil might come upon the wicked, And that Thou wouldest establish the righteous; For the righteous God trieth the heart and reins.
My shield is with God, Who saveth the upright in heart.
God is a righteous judge, Yea, a God that hath indignation every day:
If a man turn not, He will whet His sword, He hath bent His bow, and made it ready;
He hath also prepared for him the weapons of death, Yea, His arrows which He made sharp.
Behold, he travaileth with iniquity; Yea, he conceiveth mischief, and bringeth forth falsehood.
He hath digged a pit, and hollowed it, And is fallen into the ditch which he made.
His mischief shall return upon his own head, And his violence shall come down upon his own pate.
I will give thanks unto the LORD according to His righteousness; And will sing praise to the name of the LORD Most High.

Tehillim- Book of Psalms

Chapter 8
For the Leader; upon the Gittith. A Psalm of David.
O LORD, our Lord, How glorious is Thy name in all the earth! Whose majesty is rehearsed above the heavens.
Out of the mouth of babes and sucklings hast Thou founded strength, Because of Thine adversaries; That Thou mightest still the enemy and the avenger.
When I behold Thy heavens, the work of Thy fingers, The moon and the stars, which Thou hast established;
What is man, that Thou art mindful of him? And the son of man, that Thou thinkest of him?
Yet Thou hast made him but little lower than the angels, And hast crowned him with glory and honour.
Thou hast made him to have dominion over the works of Thy hands; Thou hast put all things under His feet:
Sheep and oxen, all of them, Yea, and the beasts of the field;
The fowl of the air, and the fish of the sea; Whatsoever passeth through the paths of the seas.
O LORD, our Lord, How glorious is Thy name in all the earth!

Chapter 9
For the Leader; upon Muthlabben. A Psalm of David.
I will give thanks unto the LORD with my whole heart; I will tell of all Thy marvellous works.

Tehillim- Book of Psalms

I will be glad and exult in Thee; I will sing praise to Thy name, O Most High:
When mine enemies are turned back, They stumble and perish at Thy presence;
For Thou hast maintained my right and my cause; Thou sattest upon the throne as the righteous Judge.
Thou hast rebuked the nations, Thou hast destroyed the wicked, Thou hast blotted out their name for ever and ever.
O thou enemy, the waste places are come to an end for ever; And the cities which thou didst uproot, Their very memorial is perished.
But the LORD is enthroned for ever; He hath established His throne for judgment.
And He will judge the world in righteousness, He will minister judgment to the peoples with equity.
The LORD also will be a high tower for the oppressed, A high tower in times of trouble;
And they that know Thy name will put their trust in Thee; For thou, LORD, hast not forsaken them that seek Thee.
Sing praises to the LORD, who dwelleth in Zion; Declare among the peoples His doings.
For He that avengeth blood hath remembered them; He hath not forgotten the cry of the humble.
Be gracious unto me, O LORD, Behold mine affliction at the hands of them that hate me; Thou that liftest me up from the gates of death;

Tehillim- Book of Psalms

That I may tell of all Thy praise in the gates of the daughter of Zion, That I may rejoice in Thy salvation.

The nations are sunk down in the pit that they made; In the net which they hid is their own foot taken.

The LORD hath made Himself known, He hath executed judgment, The wicked is snared in the work of his own hands. Higgaion. Selah

The wicked shall return to the nether-world, Even all the nations that forget God.

For the needy shall not alway be forgotten, Nor the expectation of the poor perish for ever.

Arise, O LORD, let not man prevail; Let the nations be judged in Thy sight.

Set terror over them, O LORD; Let the nations know they are but men. Selah.

Chapter 10

Why standest Thou afar off, O LORD? Why hidest Thou Thyself in times of trouble.

Through the pride of the wicked the poor is hotly pursued, They are taken in the devices that they have imagined.

For the wicked boasteth of his heart's desire, And the covetous vaunteth himself, though he contemn the LORD.

The wicked, in the pride of his countenance [, saith]: 'He will not require'; All his thoughts are: 'There is no God.'

Tehillim- Book of Psalms

His ways prosper at all times; Thy judgments are far above out of his sight; As for all his adversaries, he puffeth at them.

He saith in his heart: 'I shall not be moved, I who to all generations shall not be in adversity.'

His mouth is full of cursing and deceit and oppression; Under his tongue is mischief and iniquity.

He sitteth in the lurking-places of the villages; In secret places doth he slay the innocent; His eyes are on the watch for the helpless.

He lieth in wait in a secret place as a lion in his lair, He lieth in wait to catch the poor; He doth catch the poor, when he draweth him up in his net.

He croucheth, he boweth down, And the helpless fall into his mighty claws.

He hath said in his heart: 'God hath forgotten; He hideth His face; He will never see.'

Arise, O LORD; O God, lift up Thy hand; Forget not the humble.

Wherefore doth the wicked contemn God, And say in his heart: 'Thou wilt not require'?

Thou hast seen; for Thou beholdest trouble and vexation, to requite them with Thy hand; Unto Thee the helpless committeth himself; Thou hast been the helper of the fatherless.

Break Thou the arm of the wicked; And as for the evil man, search out his wickedness, till none be found.

Tehillim- Book of Psalms

The LORD is King for ever and ever; The nations are perished out of His land.

LORD, thou hast heard the desire of the humble: Thou wilt direct their heart, thou wilt cause Thine ear to attend; To right the fatherless and the oppressed, That man who is of the earth may be terrible no more.

Chapter 11

For the Leader. [A Psalm] of David. In the LORD have I taken refuge; how say ye to my soul: 'Flee thou! to your mountain, ye birds'?

For, lo, the wicked bend the bow, they have made ready their arrow upon the string, that they may shoot in darkness at the upright in heart.

When the foundations are destroyed, what hath the righteous wrought?

The LORD is in His holy temple, the LORD, His throne is in heaven; His eyes behold, His eyelids try, the children of men.

The LORD trieth the righteous; but the wicked and him that loveth violence His soul hateth.

Upon the wicked He will cause to rain coals; fire and brimstone and burning wind shall be the portion of their cup.

For the LORD is righteous, He loveth righteousness; the upright shall behold His face.

Tehillim- Book of Psalms

Chapter 12

For the Leader; on the Sheminith. A Psalm of David.

Help, LORD; for the godly man ceaseth; For the faithful fail from among the children of men.

They speak falsehood every one with his neighbour; With flattering lip, and with a double heart, do they speak.

May the LORD cut off all flattering lips, The tongue that speaketh proud things!

Who have said: 'Our tongue will we make mighty; Our lips are with us: who is lord over us?'

'For the oppression of the poor, for the sighing of the needy, Now will I arise', saith the LORD; 'I will set him in safety at whom they puff.'.

The words of the LORD are pure words, As silver tried in a crucible on the earth, refined seven times.

Thou wilt keep them, O LORD; Thou wilt preserve us from this generation for ever.

The wicked walk on every side, When vileness is exalted among the sons of men.

Chapter 13

For the Leader. A Psalm of David.

How long, O LORD, wilt Thou forget me for ever? How long wilt Thou hide Thy face from me?

How long shall I take counsel in my soul, having sorrow in my heart by day? How long shall mine enemy be exalted over me?

Tehillim- Book of Psalms

Behold Thou, and answer me, O LORD my God; Lighten mine eyes, lest I sleep the sleep of death;
Lest mine enemy say: 'I have prevailed against him'; Lest mine adversaries rejoice when I am moved.
But as for me, in Thy mercy do I trust; My heart shall rejoice in Thy salvation. I will sing unto the LORD, Because He hath dealt bountifully with me.

Chapter 14

For the Leader. [A Psalm] of David. The fool hath said in his heart: 'There is no God'; they have dealt corruptly, they have done abominably; there is none that doeth good.
The LORD looked forth from heaven upon the children of men, to see if there were any man of understanding, that did seek after God.
They are all corrupt, they are together become impure; there is none that doeth good, no, not one.
'Shall not all the workers of iniquity know it, who eat up My people as they eat bread, and call not upon the LORD?'
There are they in great fear; for God is with the righteous generation.
Ye would put to shame the counsel of the poor, but the LORD is his refuge.
Oh that the salvation of Israel were come out of Zion! When the LORD turneth the captivity of His people, let

Tehillim- Book of Psalms

Jacob rejoice, let Israel be glad.

Chapter 15
A Psalm of David. LORD, who shall sojourn in Thy tabernacle? Who shall dwell upon Thy holy mountain?
He that walketh uprightly, and worketh righteousness, And speaketh truth in his heart;
That hath no slander upon his tongue, Nor doeth evil to his fellow, Nor taketh up a reproach against his neighbour;
In whose eyes a vile person is despised, But he honoureth them that fear the LORD; He that sweareth to his own hurt, and changeth not;
He that putteth not out his money on interest, Nor taketh a bribe against the innocent. He that doeth these things shall never be moved.

Chapter 16
Michtam of David. Keep me, O God; for I have taken refuge in Thee.
I have said unto the LORD: 'Thou art my Lord; I have no good but in Thee';
As for the holy that are in the earth, They are the excellent in whom is all my delight.
Let the idols of them be multiplied that make suit unto another; Their drink-offerings of blood will I not offer, Nor take their names upon my lips.

Tehillim- Book of Psalms

O LORD, the portion of mine inheritance and of my cup, Thou maintainest my lot.

The lines are fallen unto me in pleasant places; Yea, I have a goodly heritage.

I will bless the LORD, who hath given me counsel; Yea, in the night seasons my reins instruct me.

I have set the LORD always before me; Surely He is at my right hand, I shall not be moved.

Therefore, my heart is glad, and my glory rejoiceth; my flesh also dwelleth in safety;

For Thou wilt not abandon my soul to the nether-world; Neither wilt Thou suffer Thy godly one to see the pit.

Thou makest me to know the path of life; In Thy presence is fulness of joy, In Thy right-hand bliss for evermore.

Chapter 17

A Prayer of David. Hear the right, O LORD, attend unto my cry; Give ear unto my prayer from lips without deceit.

Let my judgment come forth from Thy presence; Let Thine eyes behold equity.

Thou hast tried my heart, Thou hast visited it in the night; Thou hast tested me, and Thou findest not That I had a thought which should not pass my mouth.

As for the doings of men, by the word of Thy lips I have kept me from the ways of the violent.

My steps have held fast to Thy paths, My feet have not slipped.

Tehillim- Book of Psalms

As for me, I call upon Thee, for Thou wilt answer me, O God; Incline Thine ear unto me, hear my speech.

Make passing great Thy mercies, O Thou that savest by Thy right hand From assailants them that take refuge in Thee.

Keep me as the apple of the eye, Hide me in the shadow of Thy wings,

From the wicked that oppress, My deadly enemies, that compass me about.

Their gross heart they have shut tight, With their mouth they speak proudly.

At our every step they have now encompassed us; They set their eyes to cast us down to the earth.

He is like a lion that is eager to tear in pieces, And like a young lion lurking in secret places.

Arise, O LORD, confront him, cast him down; Deliver my soul from the wicked, by Thy sword;

From men, by Thy hand, O LORD, From men of the world, whose portion is in this life, And whose belly Thou fillest with Thy treasure; Who have children in plenty, And leave their abundance to their babes.

As for me, I shall behold Thy face in righteousness; I shall be satisfied, when I awake, with Thy likeness.

Chapter 18

For the Leader. [A Psalm] of David the servant of the LORD, who spoke unto the LORD the words of this song

Tehillim- Book of Psalms

in the day that the LORD delivered him from the hand of all his enemies, and from the hand of Saul;

And he said: I love thee, O LORD, my strength.

The LORD is my rock, and my fortress, and my deliverer; My God, my rock, in Him I take refuge; my shield, and my horn of salvation, my high tower.

Praised, I cry, is the LORD, and I am saved from mine enemies.

The cords of Death compassed me, and the floods of Belial assailed me.

The cords of Sheol surrounded me; the snares of Death confronted me.

In my distress I called upon the LORD, and cried unto my God; out of His temple He heard my voice, and my cry came before Him unto His ears.

Then the earth did shake and quake, the foundations also of the mountains did tremble; they were shaken, because He was wroth.

Smoke arose up in His nostrils, and fire out of His mouth did devour; coals flamed forth from Him.

He bowed the heavens also, and came down; and thick darkness was under His feet.

And He rode upon a cherub, and did fly; yea, He did swoop down upon the wings of the wind.

He made darkness His hiding-place, His pavilion round about Him; darkness of waters, thick clouds of the skies.

At the brightness before Him, there passed through His

Tehillim- Book of Psalms

thick clouds Hailstones and coals of fire.

The LORD also thundered in the heavens, and the Most High gave forth His voice; hailstones and coals of fire.

And He sent out His arrows, and scattered them; and He shot forth lightnings, and discomfited them.

And the channels of waters appeared, and the foundations of the world were laid bare, at Thy rebuke, O LORD, at the blast of the breath of Thy nostrils.

He sent from on high, He took me; He drew me out of many waters.

He delivered me from mine enemy most strong, and from them that hated me, for they were too mighty for me.

They confronted me in the day of my calamity; but the LORD was a stay unto me.

He brought me forth also into a large place; He delivered me, because He delighted in me.

The LORD rewarded me according to my righteousness; according to the cleanness of my hands hath He recompensed me..

For I have kept the ways of the LORD, and have not wickedly departed from my God.

For all His ordinances were before me, and I put not away His statutes from me.

And I was single-hearted with Him, and I kept myself from mine iniquity.

Therefore, hath the LORD recompensed me according to my righteousness, according to the cleanness of my hands

Tehillim- Book of Psalms

in His eyes.

With the merciful Thou dost show Thyself merciful, with the upright man Thou dost show Thyself upright;

With the pure Thou dost show Thyself pure; and with the crooked Thou dost show Thyself subtle.

For Thou dost save the afflicted people; but the haughty eyes Thou dost humble.

For Thou dost light my lamp; the LORD my God doth lighten my darkness.

For by Thee I run upon a troop; and by my God do I scale a wall.

As for God, His way is perfect; the word of the LORD is tried; He is a shield unto all them that take refuge in Him.

For who is God, save the LORD? And who is a Rock, except our God?

The God that girdeth me with strength, and maketh my way straight;

Who maketh my feet like hinds', and setteth me upon my high places;

Who traineth my hands for war, so that mine arms do bend a bow of brass.

Thou hast also given me Thy shield of salvation, and Thy right hand hath holden me up; and Thy condescension hath made me great.

Thou hast enlarged my steps under me, and my feet have not slipped.

I have pursued mine enemies, and overtaken them;

Tehillim- Book of Psalms

neither did I turn back till they were consumed.

I have smitten them through, so that they are not able to rise; they are fallen under my feet.

For Thou hast girded me with strength unto the battle; Thou hast subdued under me those that rose up against me.

Thou hast also made mine enemies turn their backs unto me, and I did cut off them that hate me.

They cried, but there was none to save; even unto the LORD, but He answered them not.

Then did I beat them small as the dust before the wind; I did cast them out as the mire of the streets.

Thou hast delivered me from the contentions of the people; Thou hast made me the head of the nations; a people whom I have not known serve me.

As soon as they hear of me, they obey me; The sons of the stranger dwindle away before me.

The sons of the stranger fade away, and come trembling out of their close places.

The LORD liveth, and blessed be my Rock; and exalted be the God of my salvation;

Even the God that executeth vengeance for me, and subdueth peoples under me.

He delivereth me from mine enemies; yea, Thou liftest me up above them that rise up against me; Thou deliverest me from the violent man.

Therefore, I will give thanks unto Thee, O LORD, among

Tehillim- Book of Psalms

the nations, and will sing praises unto Thy name.
Great salvation giveth He to His king; and showeth mercy to His anointed, To David and to his seed, for evermore.

Chapter 19

For the Leader. A Psalm of David.
The heavens declare the glory of God, and the firmament showeth His handiwork;
Day unto day uttereth speech, and night unto night revealeth knowledge;
There is no speech, there are no words, neither is their voice heard.
Their line is gone out through all the earth, and their words to the end of the world. In them hath He set a tent for the sun,
Which is as a bridegroom coming out of his chamber, and rejoiceth as a strong man to run his course.
His going forth is from the end of the heaven, and his circuit unto the ends of it; and there is nothing hid from the heat thereof.
The law of the LORD is perfect, restoring the soul; the testimony of the LORD is sure, making wise the simple..
The precepts of the LORD are right, rejoicing the heart; the commandment of the LORD is pure, enlightening the eyes.
The fear of the LORD is clean, enduring for ever; the ordinances of the LORD are true, they are righteous

Tehillim- Book of Psalms

altogether;

More to be desired are they than gold, yea, than much fine gold; sweeter also than honey and the honeycomb.

Moreover, by them is Thy servant warned; in keeping of them there is great reward.

Who can discern his errors? Clear Thou me from hidden faults.

Keep back Thy servant also from presumptuous sins, that they may not have dominion over me; then shall I be faultless, and I shall be clear from great transgression.

Let the words of my mouth and the meditation of my heart be acceptable before Thee, O LORD, my Rock, and my Redeemer.

Chapter 20

For the Leader. A Psalm of David.

The LORD answer thee in the day of trouble; The name of the God of Jacob set thee up on high;

Send forth thy help from the sanctuary, And support thee out of Zion;

Receive the memorial of all thy meal-offerings, And accept the fat of thy burnt-sacrifice; Selah

Grant thee according to thine own heart, And fulfil all thy counsel.

We will shout for joy in thy victory, And in the name of our God we will set up our standards; The LORD fulfil all thy petitions.

Tehillim- Book of Psalms

Now know I that the LORD saveth His anointed; He will answer him from His holy heaven With the mighty acts of His saving right hand.

Some trust in chariots, and some in horses; But we will make mention of the name of the LORD our God.

They are bowed down and fallen; But we are risen, and stand upright.

Save, LORD; Let the King answer us in the day that we call.

Chapter 21

For the Leader. A Psalm of David.

O LORD, in Thy strength the king rejoiceth; and in Thy salvation how greatly doth he exult!

Thou hast given him his heart's desire, and the request of his lips Thou hast not withholden. Selah

For Thou meetest him with choicest blessings; Thou settest a crown of fine gold on his head.

He asked life of Thee, Thou gavest it him; even length of days for ever and ever.

His glory is great through Thy salvation; Honour and majesty dost Thou lay upon him.

For Thou makest him most blessed for ever; Thou makest him glad with joy in Thy presence.

For the king trusteth in the LORD, yea, in the mercy of the Most High; he shall not be moved.

Tehillim- Book of Psalms

Thy hand shall be equal to all thine enemies; Thy right hand shall overtake those that hate thee.

Thou shalt make them as a fiery furnace in the time of thine anger; The LORD shall swallow them up in His wrath, and the fire shall devour them.

Their fruit shalt thou destroy from the earth, and their seed from among the children of men.

For they intended evil against thee, They imagined a device, wherewith they shall not prevail.

For thou shalt make them turn their back, Thou shalt make ready with thy bowstrings against the face of them.

Be Thou exalted, O LORD, in Thy strength; so will we sing and praise Thy power.

Chapter 22

For the Leader; upon Aijeleth ha-Shahar. A Psalm of David.

My God, my God, why hast Thou forsaken me, and art far from my help at the words of my cry?

O my God, I call by day, but Thou answerest not; and at night, and there is no surcease for me.

Yet Thou art holy, O Thou that art enthroned upon the praises of Israel.

In Thee did our fathers trust; they trusted, and Thou didst deliver them.

Unto Thee they cried, and escaped; in Thee did they trust, and were not ashamed.

Tehillim- Book of Psalms

But I am a worm, and no man; a reproach of men, and despised of the people.

All they that see me laugh me to scorn; they shoot out the lip, they shake the head:

'Let him commit himself unto the LORD! let Him rescue him; let Him deliver him, seeing He delighteth in him.'

For Thou art He that took me out of the womb; Thou madest me trust when I was upon my mother's breasts.

Upon Thee I have been cast from my birth; Thou art my God from my mother's womb.

Be not far from me; for trouble is near; for there is none to help.

Many bulls have encompassed me; strong bulls of Bashan have beset me round.

They open wide their mouth against me, as a ravening and a roaring lion.

I am poured out like water, and all my bones are out of joint; my heart is become like wax; it is melted in mine inmost parts.

My strength is dried up like a potsherd; and my tongue cleaveth to my throat; and Thou layest me in the dust of death.

For dogs have encompassed me; a company of evil-doers have inclosed me; like a lion, they are at my hands and my feet.

I may count all my bones; they look and gloat over me.

Tehillim- Book of Psalms

They part my garments among them, and for my vesture do they cast lots.
But Thou, O LORD, be not far off; O Thou my strength, hasten to help me.
Deliver my soul from the sword; mine only one from the power of the dog.
Save me from the lion's mouth; yea, from the horns of the wild-oxen do Thou answer me.
I will declare Thy name unto my brethren; in the midst of the congregation will I praise Thee.
'Ye that fear the LORD, praise Him; all ye the seed of Jacob, glorify Him; and stand in awe of Him, all ye the seed of Israel.
For He hath not despised nor abhorred the lowliness of the poor; neither hath He hid His face from him; but when he cried unto Him, He heard.'
From Thee cometh my praise in the great congregation; I will pay my vows before them that fear Him.
Let the humble eat and be satisfied; let them praise the LORD that seek after Him; may your heart be quickened for ever!
All the ends of the earth shall remember and turn unto the LORD; and all the kindreds of the nations shall worship before Thee.
For the kingdom is the LORD'S; and He is the ruler over the nations.
All the fat ones of the earth shall eat and worship; all they

Tehillim- Book of Psalms

that go down to the dust shall kneel before Him, even he that cannot keep his soul alive.

A seed shall serve him; It shall be told of the Lord unto the next generation.

They shall come and shall declare His righteousness Unto a people that shall be born, that He hath done it.

Chapter 23

A Psalm of David. The LORD is my shepherd; I shall not want.

He maketh me to lie down in green pastures; He leadeth me beside the still waters.

He restoreth my soul; He guideth me in straight paths for His name's sake.

Yea, though I walk through the valley of the shadow of death, I will fear no evil, for Thou art with me; Thy rod and Thy staff, they comfort me.

Thou preparest a table before me in the presence of mine enemies; Thou hast anointed my head with oil; my cup runneth over.

Surely goodness and mercy shall follow me all the days of my life; And I shall dwell in the house of the LORD for ever.

Chapter 24

A Psalm of David. The earth is the LORD'S, and the fulness thereof; the world, and they that dwell therein.

Tehillim- Book of Psalms

For He hath founded it upon the seas, and established it upon the floods.

Who shall ascend into the mountain of the LORD? And who shall stand in His holy place?

He that hath clean hands, and a pure heart; Who hath not taken My name in vain, and hath not sworn deceitfully.

He shall receive a blessing from the LORD, and righteousness from the God of his salvation.

Such is the generation of them that seek after Him, that seek Thy face, even Jacob. Selah

Lift up your heads, O ye gates, and be ye lifted up, ye everlasting doors; that the King of glory may come in.

'Who is the King of glory?' 'The LORD strong and mighty, The LORD mighty in battle.'

Lift up your heads, O ye gates, Yea, lift them up, ye everlasting doors; That the King of glory may come in.

'Who then is the King of glory?' 'The LORD of hosts; He is the King of glory.' Selah

Chapter 25

[A Psalm] of David. Unto Thee, O LORD, do I lift up my soul.

O my God, in Thee have I trusted, let me not be ashamed; Let not mine enemies triumph over me.

Yea, none that wait for Thee shall be ashamed; They shall be ashamed that deal treacherously without cause.

Show me Thy ways, O LORD; teach me Thy paths.

Tehillim- Book of Psalms

Guide me in Thy truth, and teach me; For Thou art the God of my salvation; For Thee do I wait all the day.

Remember, O LORD, Thy compassions and Thy mercies; For they have been from of old.

Remember not the sins of my youth, nor my transgressions; According to Thy mercy remember Thou me, For Thy goodness' sake, O LORD.

Good and upright is the LORD; Therefore, doth He instruct sinners in the way.

He guideth The humble in justice; And He teacheth the humble His way.

All the paths of the LORD are mercy and truth Unto such as keep His covenant and His testimonies.

For Thy name's sake, O LORD, Pardon mine iniquity, for it is great.

What man is he that feareth the LORD? Him will He instruct in the way that He should choose.

His soul shall abide in prosperity; And his seed shall inherit the land.

The counsel of the LORD is with them that fear Him; And His covenant, to make them know it.

Mine eyes are ever toward the LORD; For He will bring forth my feet out of the net.

Turn Thee unto me, and be gracious unto me; For I am solitary and afflicted.

The troubles of my heart are enlarged; O bring Thou me out of my distresses.

Tehillim- Book of Psalms

See mine affliction and my travail; And forgive all my sins.
Consider how many are mine enemies, And the cruel hatred wherewith they hate me..
O keep my soul, and deliver me; Let me not be ashamed, for I have taken refuge in Thee.
Let integrity and uprightness preserve me, Because I wait for Thee.
Redeem Israel, O God, out of all his troubles.

Chapter 26

A Psalm of David. Judge me, O LORD, for I have walked in mine integrity, and I have trusted in the LORD without wavering.
Examine me, O LORD, and try me; test my reins and my heart.
For Thy mercy is before mine eyes; and I have walked in Thy truth.
I have not sat with men of falsehood; neither will I go in with dissemblers.
I hate the gathering of evil doers, and will not sit with the wicked.
I will wash my hands in innocency; so, will I compass Thine altar, O LORD,
That I may make the voice of thanksgiving to be heard, and tell of all Thy wondrous works.
LORD, I love the habitation of Thy house, and the place

Tehillim- Book of Psalms

where Thy glory dwelleth.

Gather not my soul with sinners, nor my life with men of blood;

In whose hands is craftiness, and their right hand is full of bribes.

But as for me, I will walk in mine integrity; Redeem me, and be gracious unto me.

My foot standeth in an even place; in the congregations will I bless the LORD.

Chapter 27

A Psalm of David. The LORD is my light and my salvation; whom shall, I fear? The LORD is the stronghold of my life; of whom shall I be afraid?

When evil-doers came upon me to eat up my flesh, Even mine adversaries and my foes, they stumbled and fell.

Though a host should encamp against me, My heart shall not fear; Though war should rise up against me, Even then will I be confident.

One thing have I asked of the LORD, that will I seek after: That I may dwell in the house of the LORD all the days of my life, To behold the graciousness of the LORD, and to visit early in His temple.

For He concealeth me in His pavilion in the day of evil; He hideth me in the covert of His tent; He lifteth me up upon a rock.

And now shall my head be lifted up above mine enemies

Tehillim- Book of Psalms

round about me; And I will offer in His tabernacle sacrifices with trumpet-sound; I will sing, yea, I will sing praises unto the LORD.

Hear, O LORD, when I call with my voice, And be gracious unto me, and answer me.

In Thy behalf my heart hath said: 'Seek ye My face'; Thy face, LORD, will I seek.

Hide not Thy face far from me; Put not Thy servant away in anger; Thou hast been my help; Cast me not off, neither forsake me, O God of my salvation.

For though my father and my mother have forsaken me, The LORD will take me up.

Teach me Thy way, O LORD; And lead me in an even path, Because of them that lie in wait for me.

Deliver me not over unto the will of mine adversaries; For false witnesses are risen up against me, and such as breathe out violence.

If I had not believed to look upon the goodness of the LORD In the land of the living!

Wait on the LORD; Be strong, and let thy heart take courage; Yea, wait thou for the LORD.

Chapter 28

A Psalm of David. Unto thee, O LORD, do I call; My Rock, be not Thou deaf unto me; Lest, if Thou be silent unto me, I become like them that go down into the pit.

Hear the voice of my supplications, when I cry unto Thee,

Tehillim- Book of Psalms

When I lift up my hands toward Thy holy Sanctuary.

Draw me not away with the wicked, And with the workers of iniquity; Who speak peace with their neighbours, But evil is in their hearts.

Give them according to their deeds, and according to the evil of their endeavours; Give them after the work of their hands; Render to them their desert.

Because they give no heed to the works of the LORD, Nor to the operation of His hands; He will break them down and not build them up.

Blessed be the LORD, Because He hath heard the voice of my supplications.

The LORD is my strength and my shield, In Him hath my heart trusted, And I am helped; Therefore, my heart greatly rejoiceth, And with my song will I praise Him.

The LORD is a strength unto them; And He is a stronghold of salvation to His anointed.

Save Thy people, and bless Thine inheritance; And tend them, and carry them for ever.

Chapter 29

A Psalm of David. Ascribe unto the LORD, O ye sons of might, Ascribe unto the LORD glory and strength.

Ascribe unto the LORD the glory due unto His name; Worship the LORD in the beauty of holiness.

The voice of the LORD is upon the waters; The God of glory thundereth, Even the LORD upon many waters.

Tehillim- Book of Psalms

The voice of the LORD is powerful; The voice of the LORD is full of majesty.

The voice of the LORD breaketh the cedars; yea, the LORD breaketh in pieces the cedars of Lebanon.

He maketh them also to skip like a calf; Lebanon and Sirion like a young wild-ox.

The voice of the LORD heweth out flames of fire.

The voice of the LORD shaketh the wilderness; The LORD shaketh the wilderness of Kadesh.

The voice of the LORD maketh the hinds to calve, And strippeth the forests bare; And in His temple all say: 'Glory.'

The LORD sat enthroned at the flood; Yea, the LORD sitteth as King for ever.

The LORD will give strength unto His people; The LORD will bless his people with peace.

Chapter 30

A Psalm; a Song at the Dedication of the House; of David.

I will extol thee, O LORD, for Thou hast raised me up, and hast not suffered mine enemies to rejoice over me.

O LORD my God, I cried unto Thee, and Thou didst heal me;

O LORD, Thou broughtest up my soul from the nether-world; Thou didst kept me alive, that I should not go down to the pit.

Tehillim- Book of Psalms

Sing praise unto the LORD, O ye His godly ones, and give thanks to His holy name.

For His anger is but for a moment, His favour is for a lifetime; weeping may tarry for the night, but joy cometh in the morning.

Now I had said in my security: 'I shall never be moved.'

Thou hadst established, O LORD, in Thy favour my mountain as a stronghold— Thou didst hide Thy face; I was affrighted.

Unto Thee, O LORD, did I call, And unto the LORD I made supplication:

'What profit is there in my blood, when I go down to the pit? Shall the dust praise Thee? shall it declare Thy truth? Hear, O LORD, and be gracious unto me; LORD, be Thou my helper.'

Thou didst turn for me my mourning into dancing; Thou didst loose my sackcloth, and gird me with gladness;

So that my glory may sing praise to Thee, and not be silent; O LORD my God, I will give thanks unto Thee for ever.

Chapter 31

For the Leader. A Psalm of David.

In thee, O LORD, have I taken refuge; let me never be ashamed; Deliver me in Thy righteousness.

Incline Thine ear unto me, deliver me speedily; Be Thou to me a rock of refuge, even a fortress of defence, to save

Tehillim- Book of Psalms

me.
For Thou art my rock and my fortress; Therefore, for Thy name's sake lead me and guide me.
Bring me forth out of the net that they have hidden for me; For Thou art my stronghold.
Into Thy hand I commit my spirit; Thou hast redeemed me, O LORD, Thou God of truth.
I hate them that regard lying vanities; But I trust in the LORD.
I will be glad and rejoice in Thy lovingkindness; For Thou hast seen mine affliction, Thou hast taken cognizance of the troubles of my soul,
And Thou hast not given me over into the hand of the enemy; Thou hast set my feet in a broad place.
Be gracious unto me, O LORD, for I am in distress; Mine eye wasteth away with vexation, yea, my soul and my body.
For my life is spent in sorrow, and my years in sighing; My strength faileth because of mine iniquity, and my bones are wasted away.
Because of all mine adversaries I am become a reproach, Yea, unto my neighbours exceedingly, and a dread to mine acquaintance; They that see me without flee from me.
I am forgotten as a dead man out of mind; I am like a useless vessel.
For I have heard the whispering of many, Terror on every

Tehillim- Book of Psalms

side; While they took counsel together against me, They devised to take away my life.

But as for me, I have trusted in Thee, O LORD; I have said: 'Thou art my God.'

My times are in Thy hand; Deliver me from the hand of mine enemies, and from them that persecute me.

Make Thy face to shine upon Thy servant; Save me in Thy lovingkindness.

O LORD, let me not be ashamed, for I have called upon Thee; Let the wicked be ashamed, let them be put to silence in the nether-world.

Let the lying lips be dumb, Which speak arrogantly against the righteous, With pride and contempt.

Oh how abundant is Thy goodness, which Thou hast laid up for them that fear Thee; Which Thou hast wrought for them that take their refuge in Thee, in the sight of the sons of men!

Thou hidest them in the covert of Thy presence from the plottings of man; Thou concealest them in a pavilion from the strife of tongues.

Blessed be the LORD; For He hath shown me His wondrous lovingkindness in an entrenched city.

As for me, I said in my haste: 'I am cut off from before Thine eyes'; Nevertheless, Thou heardest the voice of my supplications when I cried unto Thee.

O love the LORD, all ye His godly ones; The LORD preserveth the faithful, And plentifully repayeth him that

Tehillim- Book of Psalms

acteth haughtily.

Be strong, and let your heart take courage, All ye that wait for the LORD.

Chapter 32

A Psalm of David. Maschil. Happy is he whose transgression is forgiven; whose sin is pardoned.

Happy is the man unto whom the LORD counteth not iniquity, And in whose spirit there is no guile.

When I kept silence, my bones wore away Through my groaning all the day long.

For day and night Thy hand was heavy upon me; My sap was turned as in the droughts of summer. Selah

I acknowledged my sin unto Thee, and mine iniquity have I not hid; I said: 'I will make confession concerning my transgressions unto the LORD' — And Thou, Thou forgavest the iniquity of my sin. Selah

For this let every one that is godly pray unto Thee in a time when Thou mayest be found; Surely, when the great waters overflow, they will not reach unto him.

Thou art my hiding-place; Thou wilt preserve me from the adversary; With songs of deliverance Thou wilt compass me about. Selah

'I will instruct thee and teach thee in the way which thou shalt go; I will give counsel, Mine eye being upon thee.'

Be ye not as the horse, or as the mule, which have no understanding; Whose mouth must be held in with bit and

Tehillim- Book of Psalms

bridle, That they come not near unto thee.

Many are the sorrows of the wicked; But he that trusteth in the LORD, mercy compasseth him about.

Be glad in the LORD, and rejoice, ye righteous; And shout for joy, all ye that are upright in heart.

Chapter 33

Rejoice in the LORD, O ye righteous, Praise is comely for the upright.

Give thanks unto the LORD with harp, Sing praises unto Him with the psaltery of ten strings.

Sing unto Him a new song; Play skilfully amid shouts of joy.

For the word of the LORD is upright; And all His work is done in faithfulness.

He loveth righteousness and justice; The earth is full of the lovingkindness of the LORD.

By the word of the LORD were the heavens made; And all the host of them by the breath of His mouth.

He gathereth the waters of the sea together as a heap; He layeth up the deeps in storehouses.

Let all the earth fear the LORD; Let all the inhabitants of the world stand in awe of Him.

For He spoke, and it was; He commanded, and it stood.

The LORD bringeth the counsel of the nations to nought; He maketh the thoughts of the peoples to be of no effect.

The counsel of the LORD standeth for ever, The thoughts

Tehillim- Book of Psalms

of His heart to all generations.

Happy is the nation whose God is the LORD; The people whom He hath chosen for His own inheritance.

The LORD looketh from heaven; He beholdeth all the sons of men;

From the place of His habitation He looketh intently Upon all the inhabitants of the earth;

He that fashioneth the hearts of them all, That considereth all their doings.

A king is not saved by the multitude of a host; A mighty man is not delivered by great strength.

A horse is a vain thing for safety; Neither doth it afford escape by its great strength.

Behold, the eye of the LORD is toward them that fear Him, Toward them that wait for His mercy;

To deliver their soul from death, And to keep them alive in famine.

Our soul hath waited for the LORD; He is our help and our shield.

For in Him doth our heart rejoice, Because we have trusted in His holy name.

Let Thy mercy, O LORD, be upon us, According as we have waited for Thee.

Chapter 34

[A Psalm] of David; when he changed his demeanour before Abimelech, who drove him away, and he departed.

Tehillim- Book of Psalms

I will bless the LORD at all times; His praise shall continually be in my mouth.

My soul shall glory in the LORD; The humble shall hear thereof, and be glad.

O magnify the LORD with me, And let us exalt His name together.

I sought the LORD, and He answered me, And delivered me from all my fears.

They looked unto Him, and were radiant; And their faces shall never be abashed.

This poor man cried, and the LORD heard, And saved him out of all his troubles.

The angel of the LORD encampeth round about them that fear Him, And delivereth them.

O consider and see that the LORD is good; Happy is the man that taketh refuge in Him.

O fear the LORD, ye His holy ones; For there is no want to them that fear Him.

The young lions do lack, and suffer hunger; But they that seek the LORD want not any good thing.

Come, ye children, hearken unto me; I will teach you the fear of the LORD.

Who is the man that desireth life, and loveth days, That he may see good therein?

Keep thy tongue from evil, And thy lips from speaking guile.

Depart from evil, and do good; Seek peace, and pursue it.

Tehillim- Book of Psalms

The eyes of the LORD are toward the righteous, And His ears are open unto their cry.
The face of the LORD is against them that do evil, To cut off the remembrance of them from the earth.
They cried, and the LORD heard, And delivered them out of all their troubles.
The LORD is nigh unto them that are of a broken heart, And saveth such as are of a contrite spirit.
Many are the ills of the righteous, But the LORD delivereth him out of them all.
He keepeth all his bones; Not one of them is broken.
Evil shall kill the wicked; And they that hate the righteous shall be held guilty.
The LORD redeemeth the soul of His servants; And none of them that take refuge in Him shall be desolate.

Chapter 35
[A Psalm] of David. Strive, O LORD, with them that strive with me; Fight against them that fight against me.
Take hold of shield and buckler, And rise up to my help.
Draw out also the spear, and the battle-axe, against them that pursue me; Say unto my soul: 'I am Thy salvation.'
Let them be ashamed and brought to confusion that seek after my soul; Let them be turned back and be abashed that devise my hurt.
Let them be as chaff before the wind, The angel of the LORD thrusting them.

Tehillim- Book of Psalms

Let their way be dark and slippery, The angel of the LORD pursuing them.

For without cause have they hid for me the pit, even their net, Without cause have they digged for my soul.

Let destruction come upon him unawares; And let his net that he hath hid catch himself; With destruction let him fall therein.

And my soul shall be joyful in the LORD; It shall rejoice in His salvation.

All my bones shall say: 'LORD, who is like unto Thee, Who deliverest the poor from him that is too strong for him, Yea, the poor and the needy from him that spoileth him?'

Unrighteous witnesses rise up; They ask me of things that I know not.

They repay me evil for good; Bereavement is come to my soul.

But as for me, when they were sick, my clothing was sackcloth, I afflicted my soul with fasting; And my prayer, may it return into mine own bosom.

I went about as though it had been my friend or my brother; I bowed down mournful, as one that mourneth for his mother.

But when I halt they rejoice, and gather themselves together; The abjects gather themselves together against me, and those whom I know not; They tear me, and cease not;

Tehillim- Book of Psalms

With the profanest mockeries of backbiting They gnash at me with their teeth.
Lord, how long wilt Thou look on? Rescue my soul from their destructions, Mine only one from the lions.
I will give Thee thanks in the great congregation; I will praise Thee among a numerous people.
Let not them that are wrongfully mine enemies rejoice over me; Neither let them wink with the eye that hate me without a cause.
For they speak not peace; But they devise deceitful matters against them that are quiet in the land.
Yea, they open their mouth wide against me; They say: 'Aha, aha, our eye hath seen it.'
Thou hast seen, O LORD; keep not silence; O Lord, be not far from me.
Rouse Thee, and awake to my judgment, Even unto my cause, my God and my Lord.
Judge me, O LORD my God, according to Thy righteousness; And let them not rejoice over me.
Let them not say in their heart: 'Aha, we have our desire'; Let them not say: 'We have swallowed him up.'
Let them be ashamed and abashed together that rejoice at my hurt; Let them be clothed with shame and confusion that magnify themselves against me..
Let them shout for joy, and be glad, that delight in my righteousness; Yea, let them say continually: 'Magnified be the LORD, Who delighteth in the peace of His

Tehillim- Book of Psalms

servant.'

And my tongue shall speak of Thy righteousness, And of Thy praise all the day.

Chapter 36

For the Leader. A Psalm of David the servant of the LORD.

Transgression speaketh to the wicked, methinks— There is no fear of God before his eyes.

For it flattereth him in his eyes, Until his iniquity be found, and he be hated.

The words of his mouth are iniquity and deceit; He hath left off to be wise, to do good.

He deviseth iniquity upon his bed; He setteth himself in a way that is not good; He abhorreth not evil.

Thy lovingkindness, O LORD, is in the heavens; Thy faithfulness reacheth unto the skies.

Thy righteousness is like the mighty mountains; Thy judgments are like the great deep; Man and beast Thou preservest, O LORD.

How precious is Thy lovingkindness, O God! And the children of men take refuge in the shadow of Thy wings.

They are abundantly satisfied with the fatness of Thy house; And Thou makest them drink of the river of Thy pleasures.

For with Thee is the fountain of life; In Thy light do we see light.

Tehillim- Book of Psalms

O continue Thy lovingkindness unto them that know Thee; And Thy righteousness to the upright in heart.
Let not the foot of pride overtake me, And let not the hand of the wicked drive me away.
There are the workers of iniquity fallen; They are thrust down, and are not able to rise.

Chapter 37
A Psalm of David. Fret not thyself because of evil-doers, neither be thou envious against them that work unrighteousness.
For they shall soon wither like the grass, and fade as the green herb.
Trust in the LORD, and do good; dwell in the land, and cherish faithfulness.
So shalt thou delight thyself in the LORD; and He shall give thee the petitions of thy heart.
Commit thy way unto the LORD; trust also in Him, and He will bring it to pass.
And He will make thy righteousness to go forth as the light, and thy right as the noonday.
Resign thyself unto the LORD, and wait patiently for Him; fret not thyself because of him who prospereth in his way, because of the man who bringeth wicked devices to pass.
Cease from anger, and forsake wrath; fret not thyself, it tendeth only to evil-doing.

Tehillim- Book of Psalms

For evil-doers shall be cut off; but those that wait for the LORD, they shall inherit the land.

And yet a little while, and the wicked is no more; yea, thou shalt look well at his place, and he is not.

But the humble shall inherit the land, and delight themselves in the abundance of peace.

The wicked plotteth against the righteous, and gnasheth at him with his teeth.

The Lord doth laugh at him; for He seeth that his day is coming.

The wicked have drawn out the sword, and have bent their bow; to cast down the poor and needy, to slay such as are upright in the way;

Their sword shall enter into their own heart, and their bows shall be broken.

Better is a little that the righteous hath than the abundance of many wicked.

For the arms of the wicked shall be broken; but the LORD upholdeth the righteous.

The LORD knoweth the days of them that are wholehearted; and their inheritance shall be for ever.

They shall not be ashamed in the time of evil; and in the days of famine they shall be satisfied.

For the wicked shall perish, and the enemies of the LORD shall be as the fat of lambs They shall pass away in smoke, they shall pass away.

The wicked borroweth, and payeth not; but the righteous

Tehillim- Book of Psalms

dealeth graciously, and giveth.

For such as are blessed of Him shall inherit the land; and they that are cursed of Him shall be cut off.

It is of the LORD that a man's goings are established; and He delighted in his way.

Though he fall, he shall not be utterly cast down; for the LORD upholdeth his hand.

I have been young, and now am old; yet have I not seen the righteous forsaken, nor his seed begging bread.

All the day long he dealeth graciously, and lendeth; and his seed is blessed.

Depart from evil, and do good; and dwell for evermore.

For the LORD loveth justice, And forsaketh not His saints; they are preserved for ever; but the seed of the wicked shall be cut off.

The righteous shall inherit the land, and dwell therein for ever.

The mouth of the righteous uttereth wisdom, and his tongue speaketh justice.

The law of his God is in his heart; none of his steps slide.

The wicked watcheth the righteous, and seeketh to slay him.

The LORD will not leave him in his hand, nor suffer him to be condemned when he is judged.

Wait for the LORD, and keep His way, and He will exalt thee to inherit the land; when the wicked are cut off, thou shalt see it.

Tehillim- Book of Psalms

I have seen the wicked in great power, and spreading himself like a leafy tree in its native soil.

But one passed by, and, lo, he was not; yea, I sought him, but he could not be found.

Mark the man of integrity, and behold the upright; for there is a future for the man of peace.

But transgressors shall be destroyed together; the future of the wicked shall be cut off.

But the salvation of the righteous is of the LORD; He is their stronghold in the time of trouble.

And the LORD helpeth them, and delivereth them; He delivereth them from the wicked, and saveth them, because they have taken refuge in Him.

Chapter 38

A Psalm of David, to make memorial.

O LORD, rebuke me not in Thine anger; neither chasten me in Thy wrath.

For Thine arrows are gone deep into me, and Thy hand is come down upon me.

There is no soundness in my flesh because of Thine indignation; neither is there any health in my bones because of my sin.

For mine iniquities are gone over my head; as a heavy burden they are too heavy for me.

My wounds are noisome, they fester, because of my foolishness.

Tehillim- Book of Psalms

I am bent and bowed down greatly; I go mourning all the day.
For my loins are filled with burning; and there is no soundness in my flesh.
I am benumbed and sore crushed; I groan by reason of the moaning of my heart.
Lord, all my desire is before Thee; and my sighing is not hid from Thee.
My heart fluttereth, my strength faileth me; as for the light of mine eyes, it also is gone from me.
My friends and my companions stand aloof from my plague; and my kinsmen stand afar off.
They also that seek after my life lay snares for me; and they that seek my hurt speak crafty devices, and utter deceits all the day.
But I am as a deaf man, I hear not; and I am as a dumb man that openeth not his mouth.
Yea, I am become as a man that heareth not, and in whose mouth are no arguments.
For in Thee, O LORD, do I hope; Thou wilt answer, O Lord my God.
For I said: 'Lest they rejoice over me; when my foot slippeth, they magnify themselves against me.'
For I am ready to halt, and my pain is continually before me.
For I do declare mine iniquity; I am full of care because of my sin.

Tehillim- Book of Psalms

But mine enemies are strong in health; and they that hate me wrongfully are multiplied.

They also that repay evil for good are adversaries unto me, because I follow the thing that is good.

Forsake me not, O LORD; O my God, be not far from me.

Make haste to help me, O Lord, my salvation.

Chapter 39

For the Leader, for Jeduthun. A Psalm of David.

I said: 'I will take heed to my ways, that I sin not with my tongue; I will keep a curb upon my mouth, while the wicked is before me.'

I was dumb with silence; I held my peace, had no comfort; and my pain was held in check.

My heart waxed hot within me; while I was musing, the fire kindled; Then spoke I with my tongue:

'LORD, make me to know mine end, And the measure of my days, what it is; Let me know how short-lived I am.

Behold, Thou hast made my days as hand-breadths; and mine age is as nothing before Thee; surely every man at his best estate is altogether vanity. Selah

Surely man walketh as a mere semblance; surely for vanity they are in turmoil; He heapeth up riches, and knoweth not who shall gather them.

And now, Lord, what wait I for? My hope, it is in Thee.

Deliver me from all my transgressions; make me not the reproach of the base.

Tehillim- Book of Psalms

I am dumb, I open not my mouth; because Thou hast done it.
Remove Thy stroke from off me; I am consumed by the blow of Thy hand.
With rebukes dost Thou chasten man for iniquity, and like a moth Thou makest his beauty to consume away; surely every man is vanity. Selah
Hear my prayer, O LORD, and give ear unto my cry; keep not silence at my tears; for I am a stranger with Thee, a sojourner, as all my fathers were.
Look away from me, that I may take comfort, before I go hence, and be no more.'

Chapter 40
For the Leader. A Psalm of David.
I waited patiently for the LORD; and He inclined unto me, and heard my cry.
He brought me up also out of the tumultuous pit, out of the miry clay; and He set my feet upon a rock, He established my goings.
And He hath put a new song in my mouth, even praise unto our God; many shall see, and fear, and shall trust in the LORD.
Happy is the man that hath made the LORD his trust, and hath not turned unto the arrogant, nor unto such as fall away treacherously.
Many things hast Thou done, O LORD my God, even

Tehillim- Book of Psalms

Thy wonderful works, and Thy thoughts toward us; there is none to be compared unto Thee! If I would declare and speak of them, they are more than can be told.

Sacrifice and meal-offering Thou hast no delight in; mine ears hast Thou opened; burnt-offering and sin-offering hast Thou not required.

Then said I: 'Lo, I am come with the roll of a book which is prescribed for me;

I delight to do Thy will, O my God; yea, Thy law is in my inmost parts.'

I have preached righteousness in the great congregation, Lo, I did not refrain my lips; O LORD, Thou knowest.

I have not hid Thy righteousness within my heart; I have declared Thy faithfulness and Thy salvation; I have not concealed Thy mercy and Thy truth from the great congregation.

Thou, O LORD, wilt not withhold Thy compassions from me; let Thy mercy and Thy truth continually preserve me.

For innumerable evils have compassed me about, mine iniquities have overtaken me, so that I am not able to look up; they are more than the hairs of my head, and my heart hath failed me.

Be pleased, O LORD, to deliver me; O LORD, make haste to help me.

Let them be ashamed and abashed together that seek after my soul to sweep it away; let them be turned backward and brought to confusion that delight in my hurt.

Tehillim- Book of Psalms

Let them be appalled by reason of their shame that say unto me: 'Aha, aha.'
Let all those that seek Thee rejoice and be glad in Thee; let such as love Thy salvation say continually: 'The LORD be magnified.'
But, as for me, that am poor and needy, the Lord will account it unto me; Thou art my help and my deliverer; O my God, tarry not.

Chapter 41
For the Leader. A Psalm of David.
Happy is he that considereth the poor; the LORD will deliver him in the day of evil.
The LORD preserve him, and keep him alive, let him be called happy in the land; and deliver not Thou him unto the greed of his enemies.
The LORD support him upon the bed of illness; mayest Thou turn all his lying down in his sickness.
As for me, I said: 'O LORD, be gracious unto me; heal my soul; for I have sinned against Thee.'
Mine enemies speak evil of me: 'When shall he die, and his name perish?'
And if one come to see me, he speaketh falsehood; His heart gathereth iniquity to itself; when he goeth abroad, he speaketh of it.
All that hate me whisper together against me, against me do they devise my hurt:

Tehillim- Book of Psalms

'An evil thing cleaveth fast unto him; and now that he lieth, he shall rise up no more.'
Yea, mine own familiar friend, in whom I trusted, who did eat of my bread, Hath lifted up his heel against me.
But Thou, O LORD, be gracious unto me, and raise me up, that I may requite them.
By this I know that Thou delightest in me, that mine enemy doth not triumph over me.
And as for me, Thou upholdest me because of mine integrity, and settest me before Thy face for ever.
Blessed be the LORD, the God of Israel, from everlasting and to everlasting. Amen, and Amen.

Chapter 42

For the Leader; Maschil of the sons of Korah.
As the hart panteth after the water brooks, so panteth my soul after Thee, O God.
My soul thirsteth for God, for the living God: 'When shall I come and appear before God?'
My tears have been my food day and night, while they say unto me all the day: 'Where is Thy God?'
These things I remember, and pour out my soul within me, how I passed on with the throng, and led them to the house of God, with the voice of joy and praise, a multitude keeping holyday.
Why art thou cast down, O my soul? And why moanest thou within me? Hope thou in God; for I shall yet praise

Tehillim- Book of Psalms

Him for the salvation of His countenance.

O my God, my soul is cast down within me; therefore, do I remember Thee from the land of Jordan, and the Hermons, from the hill Mizar.

Deep calleth unto deep at the voice of Thy cataracts; all Thy waves and Thy billows are gone over me.

By day the LORD will command His lovingkindness, and in the night His song shall be with me, even a prayer unto the God of my life.

I will say unto God my Rock: 'Why hast Thou forgotten me? Why go I mourning under the oppression of the enemy?'

As with a crushing in my bones, mine adversaries taunt me; while they say unto me all the day: 'Where is Thy God?'

Why art thou cast down, O my soul? And why moanest thou within me? Hope thou in God; for I shall yet praise Him, the salvation of my countenance, and my God.

Chapter 43

Be Thou my judge, O God, and plead my cause against an ungodly nation; O deliver me from the deceitful and unjust man.

For Thou art the God of my strength; why hast Thou cast me off? Why go I mourning under the oppression of the enemy?

O send out Thy light and Thy truth; let them lead me; Let

Tehillim- Book of Psalms

them bring me unto Thy holy mountain, and to Thy dwelling-places.

Then will I go unto the altar of God, unto God, my exceeding joy; And praise Thee upon the harp, O God, my God.

Why art thou cast down, O my soul? And why moanest thou within me? Hope thou in God; for I shall yet praise Him, The salvation of my countenance, and my God.

Chapter 44

For the Leader; [a Psalm] of the sons of Korah. Maschil.

O God, we have heard with our ears, our fathers have told us; a work Thou didst in their days, in the days of old.

Thou with Thy hand didst drive out the nations, and didst plant them in; Thou didst break the peoples, and didst spread them abroad.

For not by their own sword did they get the land in possession, Neither did their own arm save them; but Thy right hand, and Thine arm, and the light of Thy countenance, because Thou wast favourable unto them.

Thou art my King, O God; command the salvation of Jacob.

Through Thee do we push down our adversaries; through Thy name do we tread them under that rise up against us.

For I trust not in my bow, neither can my sword save me.

But Thou hast saved us from our adversaries, and hast put them to shame that hate us.

Tehillim- Book of Psalms

In God have we gloried all the day, and we will give thanks unto Thy name for ever. Selah

Yet Thou hast cast off, and brought us to confusion; and goest not forth with our hosts.

Thou makest us to turn back from the adversary; and they that hate us spoil at their will.

Thou hast given us like sheep to be eaten; and hast scattered us among the nations.

Thou sellest Thy people for small gain, and hast not set their prices high.

Thou makest us a taunt to our neighbours, a scorn and a derision to them that are round about us.

Thou makest us a byword among the nations, a shaking of the head among the peoples.

All the day is my confusion before me, and the shame of my face hath covered me,

For the voice of him that taunteth and blasphemeth; by reason of the enemy and the revengeful.

All this is come upon us; yet have we not forgotten Thee, neither have we been false to Thy covenant.

Our heart is not turned back, neither have our steps declined from Thy path;

Though Thou hast crushed us into a place of jackals, and covered us with the shadow of death.

If we had forgotten the name of our God, or spread forth our hands to a strange god;

Would not God search this out? For He knoweth the

Tehillim- Book of Psalms

secrets of the heart.

Nay, but for Thy sake are we killed all the day; we are accounted as sheep for the slaughter.

Awake, why sleepest Thou, O Lord? Arouse Thyself, cast not off for ever.

Wherefore hidest Thou Thy face, and forgettest our affliction and our oppression?

For our soul is bowed down to the dust; our belly cleaveth unto the earth.

Arise for our help, and redeem us for Thy mercy's sake.

Chapter 45

For the Leader; upon Shoshannim; [a Psalm] of the sons of Korah. Maschil. A Song of loves.

My heart overfloweth with a goodly matter; I say: 'My work is concerning a king'; My tongue is the pen of a ready writer.

Thou art fairer than the children of men; Grace is poured upon thy lips; Therefore, God hath blessed thee for ever.

Gird thy sword upon thy thigh, O mighty one, Thy glory and thy majesty.

And in thy majesty prosper, ride on, In behalf of truth and meekness and righteousness; And let thy right hand teach thee tremendous things.

Thine arrows are sharp The peoples fall under thee They sink into the heart of the king's enemies.

Thy throne given of God is for ever and ever; A sceptre

Tehillim- Book of Psalms

of equity is the sceptre of thy kingdom.

Thou hast loved righteousness, and hated wickedness; Therefore God, thy God, hath anointed thee With the oil of gladness above thy fellows.

Myrrh, and aloes, and cassia are all thy garments; Out of ivory palaces stringed instruments have made thee glad.

Kings' daughters are among thy favourites; At thy right hand doth stand the queen in gold of Ophir.

'Hearken, O daughter, and consider, and incline thine ear; Forget also thine own people, and thy father's house;

So shall the king desire thy beauty; For he is thy lord; and do homage unto him.

And, O daughter of Tyre, the richest of the people Shall entreat thy favour with a gift.'

All glorious is the king's daughter within the palace; Her raiment is of chequer work inwrought with gold.

She shall be led unto the king on richly woven stuff; The virgins her companions in her train being brought unto thee.

They shall be led with gladness and rejoicing; They shall enter into the king's palace.

Instead of thy fathers shall be thy sons, Whom thou shalt make princes in all the land.

I will make thy name to be remembered in all generations; Therefore, shall the peoples praise thee for ever and ever.

Tehillim- Book of Psalms

Chapter 46

For the Leader; a Psalm of the sons of Korah; upon Alamoth. A Song.

God is our refuge and strength, A very present help in trouble.

Therefore, will we not fear, though the earth do change, And though the mountains be moved into the heart of the seas;

Though the waters thereof roar and foam, Though the mountains shake at the swelling thereof. Selah

There is a river, the streams whereof make glad the city of God, The holiest dwelling-place of the Highest.

God is in the midst of her, she shall not be moved; God shall help her, at the approach of morning.

Nations were in tumult, kingdoms were moved; He uttered His voice, the earth melted.

The LORD of hosts is with us; The God of Jacob is our high tower. Selah

Come, behold the works of the LORD, Who hath made desolations in the earth.

He maketh wars to cease unto the end of the earth; He breaketh the bow, and cutteth the spear in sunder; He burneth the chariots in the fire.

'Let be, and know that I am God; I will be exalted among the nations, I will be exalted in the earth.'

The LORD of hosts is with us; The God of Jacob is our high tower. Selah.

Tehillim- Book of Psalms

Chapter 47
For the Leader; a Psalm for the sons of Korah.
O clap your hands, all ye peoples; shout unto God with the voice of triumph.
For the LORD is most high, awful; a great King over all the earth.
He subdueth peoples under us, and nations under our feet.
He chooseth our inheritance for us, the pride of Jacob whom He loveth. Selah
God is gone up amidst shouting, the LORD amidst the sound of the horn.
Sing praises to God, sing praises; sing praises unto our King, sing praises.
For God is the King of all the earth; sing ye praises in a skilful song.
God reigneth over the nations; God sitteth upon His holy throne.
The princes of the peoples are gathered together, the people of the God of Abraham; for unto God belong the shields of the earth; He is greatly exalted.

Chapter 48
A Song; a Psalm of the sons of Korah.
Great is the LORD, and highly to be praised, In the city of our God, His holy mountain,
Fair in situation, the joy of the whole earth; Even mount Zion, the uttermost parts of the north, The city of the great

Tehillim- Book of Psalms

King.

God in her palaces Hath made Himself known for a stronghold.

For, lo, the kings assembled themselves, They came onward together.

They saw, straightway they were amazed; They were affrighted, they hasted away.

Trembling took hold of them there, Pangs, as of a woman in travail.

With the east wind Thou breakest the ships of Tarshish.

As we have heard, so have we seen In the city of the LORD of hosts, in the city of our God - God establish it for ever. Selah

We have thought on Thy lovingkindness, O God, In the midst of Thy temple.

As is Thy name, O God, So is Thy praise unto the ends of the earth; Thy right hand is full of righteousness.

Let mount Zion be glad, Let the daughters of Judah rejoice, Because of Thy judgments.

Walk about Zion, and go round about her; Count the towers thereof.

Mark ye well her ramparts, Traverse her palaces; That ye may tell it to the generation following.

For such is God, our God, for ever and ever; He will guide us eternally.

Tehillim- Book of Psalms

Chapter 49

For the Leader; a Psalm for the sons of Korah.

Hear this, all ye peoples; Give ear, all ye inhabitants of the world,

Both low and high, Rich and poor together.

My mouth shall speak wisdom, and the meditation of my heart shall be understanding.

I will incline mine ear to a parable; I will open my dark saying upon the harp.

Wherefore should I fear in the days of evil, when the iniquity of my supplanters compasseth me about,

Of them that trust in their wealth, and boast themselves in the multitude of their riches?

No man can by any means redeem his brother, nor give to God a ransom for him—

For too costly is the redemption of their soul, and must be let alone for ever—

That he should still live always, that he should not see the pit.

For he seeth that wise men die, The fool and the brutish together perish, And leave their wealth to others.

Their inward thought is, that their houses shall continue for ever, And their dwelling-places to all generations; They call their lands after their own names.

But man abideth not in honour; He is like the beasts that perish.

This is the way of them that are foolish, and of those who

Tehillim- Book of Psalms

after them approve their sayings. Selah

Like sheep they are appointed for the nether-world; death shall be their shepherd; and the upright shall have dominion over them in the morning; And their form shall be for the nether-world to wear away, That there be no habitation for it.

But God will redeem my soul from the power of the nether-world; For He shall receive me. Selah

Be not thou afraid when one waxeth rich, When the wealth of his house is increased;

For when he dieth he shall carry nothing away; His wealth shall not descend after him.

Though while he lived he blessed his soul: 'Men will praise thee, when thou shalt do well to thyself';

It shall go to the generation of his fathers; They shall never see the light.

Man, that is in honour understandeth not; He is like the beasts that perish.

Chapter 50

A Psalm of Asaph. God, God, the LORD, hath spoken, and called the earth From the rising of the sun unto the going down thereof.

Out of Zion, the perfection of beauty, God hath shined forth.

Our God cometh, and doth not keep silence; a fire devoureth before Him, And round about Him it stormeth

Tehillim- Book of Psalms

mightily.
He calleth to the heavens above, and to the earth, that He may judge His people:
'Gather My saints together unto Me; those that have made a covenant with Me by sacrifice.'
And the heavens declare His righteousness; for God, He is judge. Selah
'Hear, O My people, and I will speak; O Israel, and I will testify against thee: God, thy God, am I.
I will not reprove thee for thy sacrifices; and thy burnt-offerings are continually before Me.
I will take no bullock out of thy house, nor he-goats out of thy folds.
For every beast of the forest is Mine, and the cattle upon a thousand hills.
I know all the fowls of the mountains; and the wild beasts of the field are Mine.
If I were hungry, I would not tell thee; for the world is Mine, and the fulness thereof.
Do I eat the flesh of bulls, or drink the blood of goats?
Offer unto God the sacrifice of thanksgiving; and pay thy vows unto the Highest;
And call upon Me in the day of trouble; I will deliver thee, and thou shalt honour Me.'
But unto the wicked God saith: 'What hast thou to do to declare My statutes, And that thou hast taken My covenant in thy mouth?

Tehillim- Book of Psalms

Seeing thou hatest instruction, and castest My words behind thee.

When thou sawest a thief, thou hadst company with him, and with adulterers was thy portion.

Thou hast let loose thy mouth for evil, and thy tongue frameth deceit.

Thou sittest and speakest against thy brother; Thou slanderest thine own mother's son.

These things hast thou done, and should I have kept silence? Thou hadst thought that I was altogether such a one as thyself; but I will reprove thee, and set the cause before thine eyes.

Now consider this, ye that forget God, lest I tear in pieces, and there be none to deliver.

Whoso offereth the sacrifice of thanksgiving honoureth Me; and to him that ordereth his way aright Will I show the salvation of God.'

Chapter 51

For the Leader. A Psalm of David;

when Nathan the prophet came unto him, after he had gone in to Bath-sheba.

Be gracious unto me, O God, according to Thy mercy; According to the multitude of Thy compassions blot out my transgressions.

Wash me thoroughly from mine iniquity, And cleanse me from my sin.

Tehillim- Book of Psalms

For I know my transgressions; And my sin is ever before me.

Against Thee, Thee only, have I sinned, And done that which is evil in Thy sight; That Thou mayest be justified when Thou speakest, And be in the right when Thou judgest.

Behold, I was brought forth in iniquity, and in sin did my mother conceive me.

Behold, Thou desirest truth in the inward parts; make me, therefore, to know wisdom in mine inmost heart.

Purge me with hyssop, and I shall be clean; wash me, and I shall be whiter than snow.

Make me to hear joy and gladness; that the bones which Thou hast crushed may rejoice.

Hide Thy face from my sins, and blot out all mine iniquities.

Create me a clean heart, O God; and renew a stedfast spirit within me.

Cast me not away from Thy presence; and take not Thy holy spirit from me.

Restore unto me the joy of Thy salvation; and let a willing spirit uphold me.

Then will I teach transgressors Thy ways; and sinners shall return unto Thee.

Deliver me from bloodguiltiness, O God, Thou God of my salvation; so, shall my tongue sing aloud of Thy righteousness.

Tehillim- Book of Psalms

O Lord, open Thou my lips; and my mouth shall declare Thy praise.

For Thou delightest not in sacrifice, else would I give it; Thou hast no pleasure in burnt-offering.

The sacrifices of God are a broken spirit; a broken and a contrite heart, O God, Thou wilt not despise.

Do good in Thy favour unto Zion; build Thou the walls of Jerusalem.

Then wilt Thou delight in the sacrifices of righteousness, in burnt-offering and whole offering; Then will they offer bullocks upon Thine altar.

Chapter 52

For the Leader. Maschil of David;

when Doeg the Edomite came and told Saul, and said unto him: 'David is come to the house of Ahimelech.'

Why boastest thou thyself of evil, O mighty man? The mercy of God endureth continually.

Thy tongue deviseth destruction; Like a sharp razor, working deceitfully.

Thou lovest evil more than good; Falsehood rather than speaking righteousness. Selah

Thou lovest all devouring words, The deceitful tongue.

God will likewise break thee for ever, He will take thee up, and pluck thee out of thy tent, And root thee out of the land of the living. Selah

The righteous also shall see, and fear, And shall laugh at

Tehillim- Book of Psalms

him:
'Lo, this is the man that made not God his stronghold; But trusted in the abundance of his riches, And strengthened himself in his wickedness.'

But as for me, I am like a leafy olive-tree in the house of God; I trust in the mercy of God for ever and ever.

I will give Thee thanks for ever, because Thou hast done it; And I will wait for Thy name, for it is good, in the presence of Thy saints.

Chapter 53

For the Leader; upon Mahalath. Maschil of David.

The fool hath said in his heart: 'There is no God'; They have dealt corruptly, and have done abominable iniquity; There is none that doeth good.

God looked forth from heaven upon the children of men, To see if there were any man of understanding, that did seek after God.

Every one of them is unclean, they are together become impure; There is none that doeth good, no, not one.

'Shall not the workers of iniquity know it, Who eat up My people as they eat bread, And call not upon God?'

There are they in great fear, where no fear was; For God hath scattered the bones of him that encampeth against thee; Thou hast put them to shame, because God hath rejected them.

Oh that the salvation of Israel were come out of Zion!

Tehillim- Book of Psalms

When God turneth the captivity of His people, Let Jacob rejoice, let Israel be glad.

Chapter 54

For the Leader; with string-music. Maschil of David: when the Ziphites came and said to Saul: 'Doth not David hide himself with us?'

O God, save me by Thy name, And right me by Thy might.

O God, hear my prayer; give ear to the words of my mouth.

For strangers are risen up against me, And violent men have sought after my soul; They have not set God before them. Selah

Behold, God is my helper; The Lord is for me as the upholder of my soul.

He will requite the evil unto them that lie in wait for me; Destroy Thou them in Thy truth.

With a freewill-offering will I sacrifice unto Thee; I will give thanks unto Thy name, O LORD, for it is good.

For He hath delivered me out of all trouble; And mine eye hath gazed upon mine enemies.

Chapter 55

For the Leader; with string-music. Maschil of David.

Give ear, O God, to my prayer; And hide not Thyself from my supplication.

Tehillim- Book of Psalms

Attend unto me, and hear me; I am distraught in my complaint, and will moan;
Because of the voice of the enemy, because of the oppression of the wicked; For they cast mischief upon me, and in anger they persecute me.
My heart doth writhe within me; and the terrors of death are fallen upon me.
Fear and trembling come upon me, and horror hath overwhelmed me.
And I said: 'Oh that I had wings like a dove! Then would I fly away, and be at rest.
Lo, then would I wander far off, I would lodge in the wilderness. Selah
I would haste me to a shelter from the stormy wind and tempest.'
Destroy, O Lord, and divide their tongue; For I have seen violence and strife in the city.
Day and night they go about it upon the walls thereof; iniquity also and mischief are in the midst of it.
Wickedness is in the midst thereof; oppression and guile depart not from her broad place.
For it was not an enemy that taunted me, Then I could have borne it; Neither was it mine adversary that did magnify himself against me, Then I would have hid myself from him.
But it was thou, a man mine equal, My companion, and my familiar friend;

Tehillim- Book of Psalms

We took sweet counsel together, In the house of God we walked with the throng.

May He incite death against them, Let them go down alive into the nether-world; For evil is in their dwelling, and within them.

As for me, I will call upon God; And the LORD shall save me.

Evening, and morning, and at noon, will I complain, and moan; And He hath heard my voice.

He hath redeemed my soul in peace so that none came nigh me; For they were many that strove with me.

God shall hear, and humble them, even He that is enthroned of old, Selah, such as have no changes, and fear not God.

He hath put forth his hands against them that were at peace with him; He hath profaned his covenant.

Smoother than cream were the speeches of his mouth, But his heart was war; His words were softer than oil, Yet were they keen-edged swords.

Cast thy burden upon the LORD, and He will sustain thee; He will never suffer the righteous to be moved.

But Thou, O God, wilt bring them down into the nethermost pit; Men of blood and deceit shall not live out half their days; But as for me, I will trust in Thee.

Chapter 56

For the Leader; upon Jonath-elem-rehokim. A Psalm of

Tehillim- Book of Psalms

David; Michtam; when the Philistines took him in Gath.
Be gracious unto me, O God, for man would swallow me up; All the day he fighting oppresseth me.
They that lie in wait for me would swallow me up all the day; For they are many that fight against me, O Most High,
In the day that I am afraid, I will put my trust in Thee.
In God—I will praise His word— In God do I trust, I will not be afraid; What can flesh do unto me?
All the day they trouble mine affairs; All their thoughts are against me for evil.
They gather themselves together, they hide themselves, They mark my steps; According as they have waited for my soul.
Because of iniquity cast them out; In anger bring down the peoples, O God.
Thou has counted my wanderings; Put Thou my tears into Thy bottle; Are they not in Thy book?
Then shall mine enemies turn back in the day that I call; This I know, that God is for me.
In God—I will praise His word— In the LORD—I will praise His word—
In God do I trust, I will not be afraid; What can man do unto me?
Thy vows are upon me, O God; I will render thank-offerings unto Thee.
For thou hast delivered my soul from death; Hast Thou

Tehillim- Book of Psalms

not delivered my feet from stumbling? That I may walk before God in the light of the living?

Chapter 57

For the Leader; Al-tashheth. A Psalm of David; Michtam; when he fled from Saul, in the cave.

Be gracious unto me, O God, be gracious unto me, for in Thee hath my soul taken refuge; yea, in the shadow of Thy wings will I take refuge, until calamities be overpast.

I will cry unto God Most high; unto God that accomplisheth it for me.

He will send from heaven, and save me, when he that would swallow me up taunteth, Selah; God shall send forth His mercy and His truth.

My soul is among lions, I do lie down among them that are aflame; Even the sons of men, whose teeth are spears and arrows, And their tongue a sharp sword.

Be Thou exalted, O God, above the heavens; Thy glory be above all the earth.

They have prepared a net for my steps, My soul is bowed down; They have digged a pit before me, They are fallen into the midst thereof themselves. Selah

My heart is stedfast, O God, my heart is stedfast; I will sing, yea, I will sing praises.

Awake, my glory; awake, psaltery and harp; I will awake the dawn.

I will give thanks unto Thee, O Lord, among the peoples;

Tehillim- Book of Psalms

I will sing praises unto Thee among the nations.
For Thy mercy is great unto the heavens, And Thy truth unto the skies.
Be Thou exalted, O God, above the heavens; Thy glory be above all the earth.

Chapter 58
For the Leader; Al-tashheth. A Psalm of David; Michtam.
Do ye indeed speak as a righteous company? Do ye judge with equity the sons of men?
Yea, in heart ye work wickedness; Ye weigh out in the earth the violence of your hands.
The wicked are estranged from the womb; The speakers of lies go astray as soon as they are born.
Their venom is like the venom of a serpent; They are like the deaf asp that stoppeth her ear;
Which hearkeneth not to the voice of charmers, Or of the most cunning binder of spells.
Break their teeth, O God, in their mouth; Break out the cheek-teeth of the young lions, O LORD.
Let them melt away as water that runneth apace; When he aimeth his arrows, let them be as though they were cut off.
Let them be as a snail which melteth and passeth away; Like the untimely births of a woman, that have not seen the sun.
Before your pots can feel the thorns, He will sweep it

Tehillim- Book of Psalms

away with a whirlwind, the raw and the burning alike.

The righteous shall rejoice when he seeth the vengeance; He shall wash his feet in the blood of the wicked.

And men shall say: 'Verily there is a reward for the righteous; Verily there is a God that judgeth in the earth.'

Chapter 59

For the Leader; Al-tashheth. A Psalm of David; Michtam; when Saul sent, and they watched the house to kill him.

Deliver me from mine enemies, O my God; set me on high from them that rise up against me.

Deliver me from the workers of iniquity, and save me from the men of blood.

For, lo, they lie in wait for my soul; the impudent gather themselves together against me; not for my transgression, nor for my sin, O LORD.

Without my fault, they run and prepare themselves; awake Thou to help me, and behold.

Thou therefore, O LORD God of hosts, the God of Israel, arouse Thyself to punish all the nations; show no mercy to any iniquitous traitors. Selah

They return at evening, they howl like a dog, and go round about the city.

Behold, they belch out with their mouth; swords are in their lips: 'For who doth hear?'

But Thou, O LORD, shalt laugh at them; Thou shalt have all the nations in derision.

Tehillim- Book of Psalms

Because of his strength, I will wait for Thee; for God is my high tower.

The God of my mercy will come to meet me; God will let me gaze upon mine adversaries.

Slay them not, lest my people forget, make them wander to and fro by Thy power, and bring them down, O Lord our shield.

For the sin of their mouth, and the words of their lips, let them even be taken in their pride, and for cursing and lying which, they speak.

Consume them in wrath, consume them, that they be no more; and let them know that God ruleth in Jacob, unto the ends of the earth. Selah

And they return at evening, they howl like a dog, and go round about the city;

They wander up and down to devour, and tarry all night if they have not their fill.

But as for me, I will sing of Thy strength; yea, I will sing aloud of Thy mercy in the morning; for Thou hast been my high tower, and a refuge in the day of my distress.

O my strength, unto Thee will I sing praises; for God is my high tower, the God of my mercy.

Chapter 60

For the Leader; upon Shushan Eduth; Michtam of David, to teach;

when he strove with Aram-naharaim and with Aram-

Tehillim- Book of Psalms

zobah, and Joab returned, and smote of Edom in the Valley of Salt twelve thousand.

O God, Thou hast cast us off, Thou hast broken us down; Thou hast been angry; O restore us.

Thou hast made the land to shake, Thou hast cleft it; Heal the breaches thereof; for it tottereth.

Thou hast made Thy people to see hard things; Thou hast made us to drink the wine of staggering.

Thou hast given a banner to them that fear Thee, That it may be displayed because of the truth. Selah

That Thy beloved may be delivered, Save with Thy right hand, and answer me.

God spoke in His holiness, that I would exult; That I would divide Shechem, and mete out the valley of Succoth.

Gilead is mine, and Manasseh is mine; Ephraim also is the defence of my head; Judah is my sceptre.

Moab is my washpot; Upon Edom do I cast my shoe; Philistia, cry aloud because of me!

Who will bring me into the fortified city? Who will lead me unto Edom?

Hast not Thou, O God, cast us off? And Thou goest not forth, O God, with our hosts.

Give us help against the adversary; For vain is the help of man.

Through God we shall do valiantly; For He it is that will tread down our adversaries.

Tehillim- Book of Psalms

Chapter 61

For the Leader; with string-music. [A Psalm] of David.
Hear my cry, O God; Attend unto my prayer.
From the end of the earth will I call unto Thee, when my heart fainteth; Lead me to a rock that is too high for me.
For Thou hast been a refuge for me, A tower of strength in the face of the enemy.
I will dwell in Thy Tent for ever; I will take refuge in the covert of Thy wings. Selah
For Thou, O God, hast heard my vows; Thou hast granted the heritage of those that fear Thy name..
Mayest Thou add days unto the king's days! May his years be as many generations!
May he be enthroned before God for ever! Appoint mercy and truth, that they may preserve him.
So will I sing praise unto Thy name for ever, That I may daily perform my vows.

Chapter 62

For the Leader; for Jeduthun. A Psalm of David.
Only for God doth my soul wait in stillness; From Him cometh my salvation.
He only is my rock and my salvation, My high tower, I shall not be greatly moved.
How long will ye set upon a man, That ye may slay him, all of you, As a leaning wall, a tottering fence?
They only devise to thrust him down from his height,

Tehillim- Book of Psalms

delighting in lies; They bless with their mouth, but they curse inwardly. Selah

Only for God wait thou in stillness, my soul; For from Him cometh my hope.

He only is my rock and my salvation, My high tower, I shall not be moved.

Upon God resteth my salvation and my glory; The rock of my strength, and my refuge, is in God.

Trust in Him at all times, ye people; Pour out your heart before Him; God is a refuge for us. Selah

Men of low degree are vanity, and men of high degree are a lie; If they be laid in the balances, they are together lighter than vanity.

Trust not in oppression, And put not vain hope in robbery; If riches increase, set not your heart thereon.

God hath spoken once, Twice have I heard this: That strength belongeth unto God;

Also unto Thee, O Lord, belongeth mercy; For Thou renderest to every man according to his work.

Chapter 63

A Psalm of David, when he was in the wilderness of Judah.

O God, Thou art my God, earnestly will I seek Thee; My soul thirsteth for Thee, my flesh longeth for Thee, In a dry and weary land, where no water is.

So have I looked for Thee in the sanctuary, To see Thy

Tehillim- Book of Psalms

power and Thy glory.

For Thy lovingkindness is better than life; My lips shall praise Thee.

So will I bless Thee as long as I live; In Thy name will I lift up my hands.

My soul is satisfied as with marrow and fatness; And my mouth doth praise Thee with joyful lips;

When I remember Thee upon my couch, And meditate on Thee in the night-watches.

For Thou hast been my help, And in the shadow of Thy wings do I rejoice.

My soul cleaveth unto Thee; Thy right hand holdeth me fast.

But those that seek my soul, to destroy it, Shall go into the nethermost parts of the earth.

They shall be hurled to the power of the sword; They shall be a portion for foxes.

But the king shall rejoice in God; Every one that sweareth by Him shall glory; For the mouth of them that speak lies shall be stopped.

Chapter 64

For the Leader. A Psalm of David.

Hear my voice, O God, in my complaint; preserve my life from the terror of the enemy.

Hide me from the council of evil-doers; from the tumult of the workers of iniquity;

Tehillim- Book of Psalms

Who have whet their tongue like a sword, and have aimed their arrow, a poisoned word;

That they may shoot in secret places at the blameless; suddenly do they shoot at him, and fear not.

They encourage one another in an evil matter; they converse of laying snares secretly; they ask, who would see them.

They search out iniquities, they have accomplished a diligent search; even in the inward thought of every one, and the deep heart.

But God doth shoot at them with an arrow suddenly; thence are their wounds.

So they make their own tongue a stumbling unto themselves; all that see them shake the head.

And all men fear; and they declare the work of God, and understand His doing.

The righteous shall be glad in the LORD, and shall take refuge in Him; and all the upright in heart shall glory.

Chapter 65

For the Leader. A Psalm. A Song of David.

Praise waiteth for Thee, O God, in Zion; and unto Thee the vow is performed.

O Thou that hearest prayer, unto Thee doth all flesh come.

The tale of iniquities is too heavy for me; as for our transgressions, Thou wilt pardon them.

Happy is the man whom Thou choosest, and bringest

Tehillim- Book of Psalms

near, that he may dwell in Thy courts; may we be satisfied with the goodness of Thy house, the holy place of Thy temple!

With wondrous works dost Thou answer us in righteousness, O God of our salvation; Thou the confidence of all the ends of the earth, and of the far distant seas;

Who by Thy strength settest fast the mountains, who art girded about with might;

Who stillest the roaring of the seas, the roaring of their waves, and the tumult of the peoples;

So that they that dwell in the uttermost parts stand in awe of Thy signs; Thou makest the outgoings of the morning and evening to rejoice.

Thou hast remembered the earth, and watered her, greatly enriching her, with the river of God that is full of water; Thou preparest them corn, for so preparest Thou her.

Watering her ridges abundantly, settling down the furrows thereof, Thou makest her soft with showers; Thou blessest the growth thereof.

Thou crownest the year with Thy goodness; and Thy paths drop fatness.

The pastures of the wilderness do drop; and the hills are girded with joy.

The meadows are clothed with flocks; the valleys also are covered over with corn; they shout for joy, yea, they sing.

Tehillim- Book of Psalms

Chapter 66

For the Leader. A Song, a Psalm. Shout unto God, all the earth;

Sing praises unto the glory of His name; Make His praise glorious.

Say unto God: 'How tremendous is Thy work! Through the greatness of Thy power shall Thine enemies dwindle away before Thee.

All the earth shall worship Thee, And shall sing praises unto Thee; They shall sing praises to Thy name.' Selah

Come, and see the works of God; He is terrible in His doing toward the children of men.

He turned the sea into dry land; They went through the river on foot; There let us rejoice in Him!

Who ruleth by His might for ever; His eyes keep watch upon the nations; Let not the rebellious exalt themselves? Selah

Bless our God, ye peoples, And make the voice of His praise to be heard;

Who hath set our soul in life, And suffered not our foot to be moved,

For Thou, O God, hast tried us; Thou hast refined us, as silver is refined.

Thou didst bring us into the hold; Thou didst lay constraint upon our loins.

Thou hast caused men to ride over our heads; We went through fire and through water; But Thou didst bring us

Tehillim- Book of Psalms

out unto abundance.
I will come into Thy house with burnt-offerings, I will perform unto Thee my vows,
Which my lips have uttered, And my mouth hath spoken, when I was in distress.
I will offer unto Thee burnt-offerings of fatlings, With the sweet smoke of rams; I will offer bullocks with goats. Selah
Come, and hearken, all ye that fear God, And I will declare what He hath done for my soul.
I cried unto Him with my mouth, And He was extolled with my tongue.
If I had regarded iniquity in my heart, The Lord would not hear;
But verily God hath heard; He hath attended to the voice of my prayer.
Blessed be God, Who hath not turned away my prayer, nor His mercy from me.

Chapter 67

For the Leader; with string-music. A Psalm, a Song.
God be gracious unto us, and bless us; May He cause His face to shine toward us; Selah.
That Thy way may be known upon earth, Thy salvation among all nations.
Let the peoples give thanks unto Thee, O God; Let the peoples give thanks unto Thee, all of them.

Tehillim- Book of Psalms

O let the nations be glad and sing for joy; For Thou wilt judge the peoples with equity, And lead the nations upon earth. Selah.

Let the peoples give thanks unto Thee, O God; Let the peoples give thanks unto Thee, all of them.

The earth hath yielded her increase; May God, our own God, bless us.

May God bless us; And let all the ends of the earth fear Him.

Chapter 68

For the Leader. A Psalm of David, a Song.

Let God arise, let His enemies be scattered; And let them that hate Him flee before Him.

As smoke is driven away, so drive them away; As wax melteth before the fire, So, let the wicked perish at the presence of God.

But let the righteous be glad, let them exult before God; Yea, let them rejoice with gladness.

Sing unto God, sing praises to His name; Extol Him that rideth upon the skies, whose name is the LORD; And exult ye before Him.

A father of the fatherless, and a judge of the widows, Is God in His holy habitation.

God maketh the solitary to dwell in a house; He bringeth out the prisoners into prosperity; The rebellious dwell but in a parched land.

Tehillim- Book of Psalms

O God, when Thou wentest forth before Thy people, When Thou didst march through the wilderness; Selah

The earth trembled, the heavens also dropped at the presence of God; Even yon Sinai trembled at the presence of God, the God of Israel.

A bounteous rain didst Thou pour down, O God; When Thine inheritance was weary, Thou didst confirm it.

Thy flock settled therein; Thou didst prepare in Thy goodness for the poor, O God.

The Lord giveth the word; The women that proclaim the tidings are a great host.

Kings of armies flee, they flee; And she that tarrieth at home divideth the spoil.

When ye lie among the sheepfolds, The wings of the dove are covered with silver, And her pinions with the shimmer of gold.

When the Almighty scattereth kings therein, It snoweth in Zalmon.

A mountain of God is the mountain of Bashan; A mountain of peaks is the mountain of Bashan.

Why look ye askance, ye mountains of peaks, At the mountain which God hath desired for His abode? Yea, the LORD will dwell therein for ever.

The chariots of God are myriads, even thousands upon thousands; The Lord is among them, as in Sinai, in holiness.

Thou hast ascended on high, Thou hast led captivity

Tehillim- Book of Psalms

captive; Thou hast received gifts among men, Yea, among the rebellious also, that the LORD God might dwell there.

Blessed be the Lord, day by day He beareth our burden, Even the God who is our salvation. Selah

God is unto us a God of deliverances; And unto GOD the Lord belong the issues of death.

Surely God will smite through the head of His enemies, The hairy scalp of him that goeth about in his guiltiness.

The Lord said: 'I will bring back from Bashan, I will bring them back from the depths of the sea;

That thy foot may wade through blood, That the tongue of thy dogs may have its portion from thine enemies.'

They see Thy goings, O God, Even the goings of my God, my King, in holiness.

The singers go before, the minstrels follow after, In the midst of damsels playing upon timbrels.

'Bless ye God in full assemblies, Even the Lord, ye that are from the fountain of Israel.'

There is Benjamin, the youngest, ruling them, The princes of Judah their council, The princes of Zebulun, the princes of Naphtali.

Thy God hath commanded thy strength; Be strong, O God, Thou that hast wrought for us

Out of Thy temple at Jerusalem, Whither kings shall bring presents unto Thee.

Rebuke the wild beast of the reeds, The multitude of the

Tehillim- Book of Psalms

bulls, with the calves of the peoples, Every one submitting himself with pieces of silver; He hath scattered the peoples that delight in war!

Nobles shall come out of Egypt; Ethiopia shall hasten to stretch out her hands unto God.

Sing unto God, ye kingdoms of the earth; O sing praises unto the Lord; Selah

To Him that rideth upon the heavens of heavens, which are of old; Lo, He uttereth His voice, a mighty voice.

Ascribe ye strength unto God; His majesty is over Israel, And His strength is in the skies.

Awful is God out of thy holy places; The God of Israel, He giveth strength and power unto the people; Blessed be God.

Chapter 69

For the Leader; upon Shoshannim. A Psalm of David.

Save me, O God; For the waters are come in even unto the soul.

I am sunk in deep mire, where there is no standing; I am come into deep waters, and the flood overwhelmeth me.

I am weary of my crying; my throat is dried; Mine eyes fail while I wait for my God.

They that hate me without a cause are more than the hairs of my head; They that would cut me off, being mine enemies wrongfully, are many; Should I restore that which I took not away?

Tehillim- Book of Psalms

O God, Thou knowest my folly; And my trespasses are not hid from Thee.

Let not them that wait for Thee be ashamed through me, O Lord GOD of hosts; Let not those that seek Thee be brought to confusion through me, O God of Israel.

Because for Thy sake I have borne reproach; Confusion hath covered my face.

I am become a stranger unto my brethren, And an alien unto my mother's children.

Because zeal for Thy house hath eaten me up, And the reproaches of them that reproach Thee are fallen upon me.

And I wept with my soul with fasting, And that became unto me a reproach.

I made sackcloth also my garment, And I became a byword unto them.

They that sit in the gate talk of me; And I am the song of the drunkards.

But as for me, let my prayer be unto Thee, O LORD, in an acceptable time; O God, in the abundance of Thy mercy, Answer me with the truth of Thy salvation.

Deliver me out of the mire, and let me not sink; Let me be delivered from them that hate me, and out of the deep waters.

Let not the waterflood overwhelm me, Neither let the deep swallow me up; And let not the pit shut her mouth upon me.

Tehillim- Book of Psalms

Answer me, O LORD, for Thy mercy is good; According to the multitude of Thy compassions turn Thou unto me.

And hide not Thy face from Thy servant; For I am in distress; answer me speedily.

Draw nigh unto my soul, and redeem it; Ransom me because of mine enemies.

Thou knowest my reproach, and my shame, and my confusion; Mine adversaries are all before Thee.

Reproach hath broken my heart; and I am sore sick; And I looked for some to show compassion, but there was none; And for comforters, but I found none.

Yea, they put poison into my food; And in my thirst they gave me vinegar to drink.

Let their table before them become a snare; And when they are in peace, let it become a trap.

Let their eyes be darkened, that they see not; And make their loins continually to totter.

Pour out Thine indignation upon them, And let the fierceness of Thine anger overtake them.

Let their encampment be desolate; Let none dwell in their tents.

For they persecute him whom Thou hast smitten; And they tell of the pain of those whom Thou hast wounded.

Add iniquity unto their iniquity; And let them not come into Thy righteousness.

Let them be blotted out of the book of the living, And not be written with the righteous.

Tehillim- Book of Psalms

But I am afflicted and in pain; Let Thy salvation, O God, set me up on high.

I will praise the name of God with a song, And will magnify Him with thanksgiving.

And it shall please the LORD better than a bullock That hath horns and hoofs.

The humble shall see it, and be glad; Ye that seek after God, let your heart revive.

For the LORD hearkeneth unto the needy, And despiseth not His prisoners.

Let heaven and earth praise Him, The seas, and every thing that moveth therein.

For God will save Zion, and build the cities of Judah; And they shall abide there, and have it in possession.

The seed also of His servants shall inherit it; And they that love His name shall dwell therein.

Chapter 70

For the Leader. [A Psalm] of David; to make memorial.

O God, to deliver me, O LORD, to help me, make haste.

Let them be ashamed and abashed That seek after my soul; Let them be turned backward and brought to confusion That delight in my hurt.

Let them be turned back by reason of their shame That say: 'Aha, aha.'

Let all those that seek Thee rejoice and be glad in Thee; And let such as love Thy salvation say continually: 'Let

Tehillim- Book of Psalms

God be magnified.'
But I am poor and needy; O God, make haste unto me;
Thou art my help and my deliverer; O LORD, tarry not.

Chapter 71
In Thee, O LORD, have I taken refuge; Let me never be ashamed.
Deliver me in Thy righteousness, and rescue me; Incline Thine ear unto me, and save me.
Be Thou to me a sheltering rock, whereunto I may continually resort, Which Thou hast appointed to save me; For Thou art my rock and my fortress.
O my God, rescue me out of the hand of the wicked, Out of the grasp of the unrighteous and ruthless man.
For Thou art my hope; O Lord GOD, my trust from my youth.
Upon Thee have I stayed myself from birth; Thou art he that took me out of my mother's womb; My praise is continually of Thee.
I am as a wonder unto many; But Thou art my strong refuge.
My mouth shall be filled with Thy praise, And with Thy glory all the day.
Cast me not off in the time of old age; When my strength faileth, forsake me not.
For mine enemies speak concerning me, And they that watch for my soul take counsel together,

Tehillim- Book of Psalms

Saying: 'God hath forsaken him; Pursue and take him; for there is none to deliver.'

O God, be not far from me; O my God, make haste to help me.

Let them be ashamed and consumed that are adversaries to my soul; Let them be covered with reproach and confusion that seek my hurt.

But as for me, I will hope continually, And will praise Thee yet more and more.

My mouth shall tell of Thy righteousness, And of Thy salvation all the day; For I know not the numbers thereof.

I will come with Thy mighty acts, O Lord GOD; I will make mention of Thy righteousness, even of Thine only.

O God, Thou hast taught me from my youth; And until now do I declare Thy wondrous works.

And even unto old age and hoary hairs, O God, forsake me not; Until I have declared Thy strength unto the next generation, Thy might to every one that is to come.

Thy righteousness also, O God, which reacheth unto high heaven; Thou who hast done great things, O God, who is like unto Thee?

Thou, who hast made me to see many and sore troubles, Wilt quicken me again, and bring me up again from the depths of the earth.

Thou wilt increase my greatness, And turn and comfort me.

I also will give thanks unto Thee with the psaltery, Even

Tehillim- Book of Psalms

unto Thy truth, O my God; I will sing praises unto Thee with the harp, O Thou Holy One of Israel.

My lips shall greatly rejoice when I sing praises unto Thee; And my soul, which Thou hast redeemed.

My tongue also shall tell of Thy righteousness all the day; For they are ashamed, for they are abashed, that seek my hurt.

Chapter 72

[A Psalm] of Solomon. Give the king Thy judgments, O God, and Thy righteousness unto the king's son;

That he may judge Thy people with righteousness, and Thy poor with justice.

Let the mountains bear peace to the people, and the hills, through righteousness.

May he judge the poor of the people, and save the children of the needy, And crush the oppressor.

They shall fear Thee while the sun endureth, and so long as the moon, throughout all generations.

May he come down like rain upon the mown grass, as showers that water the earth.

In his days let the righteous flourish, and abundance of peace, till the moon be no more.

May he have dominion also from sea to sea, and from the River unto the ends of the earth.

Let them that dwell in the wilderness bow before him; and his enemies lick the dust.

Tehillim- Book of Psalms

The kings of Tarshish and of the isles shall render tribute; the kings of Sheba and Seba shall offer gifts.

Yea, all kings shall prostrate themselves before him; All nations shall serve him.

For he will deliver the needy when he crieth; the poor also, and him that hath no helper.

He will have pity on the poor and needy, And the souls of the needy he will save.

He will redeem their soul from oppression and violence, And precious will their blood be in his sight.

That they may live, and that he may give them of the gold of Sheba, That they may pray for him continually, Yea, bless him all the day.

May he be as a rich cornfield in the land upon the top of the mountains; May his fruit rustle like Lebanon; And may they blossom out of the city like grass of the earth.

May his name endure for ever; May his name be continued as long as the sun; May men also bless themselves by him; May all nations call him happy.

Blessed be the LORD God, the God of Israel, Who only doeth wondrous things;

And blessed be His glorious name for ever; And let the whole earth be filled with His glory. Amen, and Amen.

The prayers of David the son of Jesse are ended.

Chapter 73

A Psalm of Asaph. Surely God is good to Israel, even to

Tehillim- Book of Psalms

such as are pure in heart.

But as for me, my feet were almost gone; my steps had well nigh slipped.

For I was envious at the arrogant, when I saw the prosperity of the wicked.

For there are no pangs at their death, and their body is sound.

In the trouble of man they are not; neither are they plagued like men.

Therefore, pride is as a chain about their neck; violence covereth them as a garment.

Their eyes stand forth from fatness; they are gone beyond the imaginations of their heart.

They scoff, and in wickedness utter oppression; they speak as if there were none on high.

They have set their mouth against the heavens, And their tongue walketh through the earth.

Therefore, His people return hither; And waters of fullness are drained out by them.

And they say: 'How doth God know? And is there knowledge in the Highest?'

Behold, such are the wicked; And they that are always at ease increase riches.

Surely in vain have I cleansed my heart, And washed my hands in innocency;

For all the day have I been plagued, And my chastisement came every morning.

Tehillim- Book of Psalms

If I had said: 'I will speak thus', Behold, I had been faithless to the generation of Thy children.

And when I pondered how I might know this, It was wearisome in mine eyes;

Until I entered into the sanctuary of God, And considered their end.

Surely, Thou settest them in slippery places; Thou hurlest them down to utter ruin.

How are they become a desolation in a moment! They are wholly consumed by terrors.

As a dream when one awaketh, So, O Lord, when Thou arousest Thyself, Thou wilt despise their semblance.

For my heart was in a ferment, And I was pricked in my reins.

But I was brutish, and ignorant; I was as a beast before Thee.

Nevertheless, I am continually with Thee; Thou holdest my right hand.

Thou wilt guide me with Thy counsel, And afterward receive me with glory.

Whom have I in heaven but Thee? And beside Thee I desire none upon earth.

My flesh and my heart faileth; But God is the rock of my heart and my portion for ever.

For, lo, they that go far from Thee shall perish; Thou dost destroy all them that go astray from Thee.

But as for me, the nearness of God is my good; I have

Tehillim- Book of Psalms

made the Lord GOD my refuge, That I may tell of all Thy works.

Chapter 74

Maschil of Asaph. Why, O God, hast Thou cast us off for ever? Why doth Thine anger smoke against the flock of Thy pasture?

Remember Thy congregation, which Thou hast gotten of old, Which Thou hast redeemed to be the tribe of Thine inheritance; And mount Zion, wherein Thou hast dwelt.

Lift up Thy steps because of the perpetual ruins, Even all the evil that the enemy hath done in the sanctuary.

Thine adversaries have roared in the midst of Thy meeting-place; They have set up their own signs for signs.

It seemed as when men wield upwards Axes in a thicket of trees.

And now all the carved work thereof together They strike down with hatchet and hammers.

They have set Thy sanctuary on fire; They have profaned the dwelling-place of Thy name even to the ground.

They said in their heart: 'Let us make havoc of them altogether'; They have burned up all the meeting-places of God in the land.

We see not our signs; There is no more any prophet; Neither is there among us any that knoweth how long.

How long, O God, shall the adversary reproach? Shall the

Tehillim- Book of Psalms

enemy blaspheme Thy name for ever?

Why withdrawest Thou Thy hand, even Thy right hand? Draw it out of Thy bosom and consume them.

Yet God is my King of old, Working salvation in the midst of the earth.

Thou didst break the sea in pieces by Thy strength; Thou didst shatter the heads of the sea-monsters in the waters.

Thou didst crush the heads of leviathan, Thou gavest him to be food to the folk inhabiting the wilderness.

Thou didst cleave fountain and brook; Thou driedst up ever-flowing rivers.

Thine is the day, Thine also the night; Thou hast established luminary and sun.

Thou hast set all the borders of the earth; Thou hast made summer and winter.

Remember this, how the enemy hath reproached the LORD, And how a base people have blasphemed Thy name.

O deliver not the soul of Thy turtle-dove unto the wild beast; Forget not the life of Thy poor for ever.

Look upon the covenant; For the dark places of the land are full of the habitations of violence.

O let not the oppressed turn back in confusion; Let the poor and needy praise Thy name.

Arise, O God, plead Thine own cause; Remember Thy reproach all the day at the hand of the base man.

Forget not the voice of Thine adversaries, The tumult of

Tehillim- Book of Psalms

those that rise up against Thee which ascendeth continually.

Chapter 75

For the Leader; Al-tashheth. A Psalm of Asaph, a Song.

We give thanks unto Thee, O God, We give thanks, and Thy name is near; Men tell of Thy wondrous works.

'When I take the appointed time, I Myself will judge with equity.

When the earth and all the inhabitants thereof are dissolved, I Myself establish the pillars of it.' Selah

I say unto the arrogant 'Deal not arrogantly'; And to the wicked 'Lift not up the horn.'

Lift not up your horn on high; Speak not insolence with a haughty neck.

For neither from the east, nor from the west, Nor yet from the wilderness, cometh lifting up.

For God is judge; He putteth down one, and lifteth up another.

For in the hand of the LORD there is a cup, with foaming wine, full of mixture, And He poureth out of the same; Surely the dregs thereof, all the wicked of the earth shall drain them, and drink them.

But as for me, I will declare for ever, I will sing praises to the God of Jacob.

All the horns of the wicked also will I cut off; But the horns of the righteous shall be lifted up.

Tehillim- Book of Psalms

Chapter 76

For the Leader; with string-music. A Psalm of Asaph, a Song.

In Judah is God known; His name is great in Israel.

In Salem also is set His tabernacle, And His dwelling-place in Zion.

There He broke the fiery shafts of the bow; The shield, and the sword, and the battle. Selah

Glorious art Thou and excellent, coming down from the mountains of prey.

The stout-hearted are bereft of sense, they sleep their sleep; And none of the men of might have found their hands.

At Thy rebuke, O God of Jacob, They are cast into a dead sleep, the riders also and the horses.

Thou, even Thou, art terrible; And who may stand in Thy sight when once Thou art angry?

Thou didst cause sentence to be heard from heaven; The earth feared, and was still,

When God arose to judgment, To save all the humble of the earth. Selah

Surely the wrath of man shall praise Thee; The residue of wrath shalt Thou gird upon Thee.

Vow, and pay unto the LORD your God; Let all that are round about Him bring presents unto Him that is to be feared;

He minisheth the spirit of princes; He is terrible to the

Tehillim- Book of Psalms

kings of the earth.

Chapter 77
For the Leader; for Jeduthun. A Psalm of Asaph.
I will lift up my voice unto God, a cry; I will lift up my voice unto God, that He may give ear unto me.
In the day of my trouble I seek the Lord; With my hand uplifted, [mine eye] streameth in the night without ceasing; My soul refuseth to be comforted.
When I think thereon, O God, I must moan; When I muse thereon, my spirit fainteth. Selah.
Thou holdest fast the lids of mine eyes; I am troubled, and cannot speak.
I have pondered the days of old, the years of ancient times.
In the night I will call to remembrance my song; I will commune with mine own heart; And my spirit maketh diligent search
'Will the Lord cast off for ever? And will He be favourable no more?
Is His mercy clean gone for ever? Is His promise come to an end for evermore?
Hath God forgotten to be gracious? Hath He in anger shut up his compassions?' Selah
And I say 'This is my weakness, That the right hand of the Most High could change.
I will make mention of the deeds of the LORD; Yea, I

Tehillim- Book of Psalms

will remember Thy wonders of old.

I will meditate also upon all Thy work, And muse on Thy doings.'

O God, Thy way is in holiness; Who is a great god like unto God?

Thou art the God that doest wonders; Thou hast made known Thy strength among the peoples.

Thou hast with Thine arm redeemed Thy people, The sons of Jacob and Joseph. Selah

The waters saw Thee, O God; The waters saw Thee, they were in pain; The depths also trembled.

The clouds flooded forth waters; The skies sent out a sound; Thine arrows also went abroad.

The voice of Thy thunder was in the whirlwind; The lightnings lighted up the world; The earth trembled and shook.

Thy way was in the sea, And Thy path in the great waters, And Thy footsteps were not known.

Thou didst lead Thy people like a flock, By the hand of Moses and Aaron.

Chapter 78

Maschil of Asaph. Give ear, O my people, to my teaching; Incline your ears to the words of my mouth.

I will open my mouth with a parable; I will utter dark sayings concerning days of old;

That which we have heard and known, And our fathers

Tehillim- Book of Psalms

have told us,

We will not hide from their children, Telling to the generation to come the praises of the LORD, And His strength, and His wondrous works that He hath done.

For He established a testimony in Jacob, And appointed a law in Israel, Which He commanded our fathers, That they should make them known to their children;

That the generation to come might know them, even the children that should be born; Who should arise and tell them to their children,

That they might put their confidence in God, And not forget the works of God, But keep His commandments;

And might not be as their fathers, A stubborn and rebellious generation; A generation that set not their heart aright, And whose spirit was not stedfast with God.

The children of Ephraim were as archers handling the bow, That turned back in the day of battle.

They kept not the covenant of God, And refused to walk in His law;

And they forgot His doings, And His wondrous works that He had shown them.

Marvellous things did He in the sight of their fathers, In the land of Egypt, in the field of Zoan.

He cleaved the sea, and caused them to pass through; And He made the waters to stand as a heap.

By day also He led them with a cloud, And all the night with a light of fire.

Tehillim- Book of Psalms

He cleaved rocks in the wilderness, And gave them drink abundantly as out of the great deep.

He brought streams also out of the rock, And caused waters to run down like rivers.

Yet went they on still to sin against Him, To rebel against the Most High in the desert.

And they tried God in their heart By asking food for their craving.

Yea, they spoke against God; They said 'Can God prepare a table in the wilderness?

Behold, He smote the rock, that waters gushed out, And streams overflowed; Can He give bread also? Or will He provide flesh for His people?'

Therefore, the LORD heard, and was wroth; And a fire was kindled against Jacob, And anger also went up against Israel;

Because they believed not in God, And trusted not in His salvation.

And He commanded the skies above, And opened the doors of heaven;

And He caused manna to rain upon them for food, And gave them of the corn of heaven.

Man did eat the bread of the mighty; He sent them provisions to the full.

He caused the east wind to set forth in heaven; And by His power He brought on the south wind.

He caused flesh also to rain upon them as the dust, And

Tehillim- Book of Psalms

winged fowl as the sand of the seas;
And He let it fall in the midst of their camp, Round about their dwellings.
So, they did eat, and were well filled; And He gave them that which they craved.
They were not estranged from their craving, Their food was yet in their mouths,
When the anger of God went up against them, And slew of the lustieth among them, And smote down the young men of Israel.
For all this they sinned still, And believed not in His wondrous works.
Therefore, He ended their days as a breath, And their years in terror.
When He slew them, then they would inquire after Him, And turn back and seek God earnestly.
And they remembered that God was their Rock, And the Most High God their redeemer.
But they beguiled Him with their mouth, And lied unto Him with their tongue.
For their heart was not stedfast with Him, Neither were they faithful in His covenant.
But He, being full of compassion, forgiveth iniquity, and destroyeth not; Yea, many a time doth He turn His anger away, And doth not stir up all His wrath.
So He remembered that they were but flesh, A wind that passeth away, and cometh not again.

Tehillim- Book of Psalms

How oft did they rebel against Him in the wilderness, And grieve Him in the desert!

And still again they tried God, And set bounds to the Holy One of Israel.

They remembered not His hand, Nor the day when He redeemed them from the adversary.

How He set His signs in Egypt, And His wonders in the field of Zoan;.

And turned their rivers into blood, So that they could not drink their streams.

He sent among them swarms of flies, which devoured them; And frogs, which destroyed them.

He gave also their increase unto the caterpillar, And their labour unto the locust.

He destroyed their vines with hail, And their sycamore-trees with frost.

He gave over their cattle also to the hail, And their flocks to fiery bolts.

He sent forth upon them the fierceness of His anger, Wrath, and indignation, and trouble, A sending of messengers of evil.

He levelled a path for His anger; He spared not their soul from death, But gave their life over to the pestilence;

And smote all the first-born in Egypt, The first-fruits of their strength in the tents of Ham;

But He made His own people to go forth like sheep, And guided them in the wilderness like a flock.

Tehillim- Book of Psalms

And He led them safely, and they feared not; But the sea overwhelmed their enemies.

And He brought them to His holy border, To the mountain, which His right hand had gotten.

He drove out the nations also before them, And allotted them for an inheritance by line, And made the tribes of Israel to dwell in their tents.

Yet they tried and provoked God, the Most High, And kept not His testimonies;

But turned back, and dealt treacherously like their fathers; They were turned aside like a deceitful bow.

For they provoked Him with their high places, And moved Him to jealousy with their graven images.

God heard, and was wroth, And He greatly abhorred Israel;

And He forsook the tabernacle of Shiloh, The tent which He had made to dwell among men;

And delivered His strength into captivity, And His glory into the adversary's hand.

He gave His people over also unto the sword; And was wroth with His inheritance.

Fire devoured their young men; And their virgins had no marriage-song.

Their priests fell by the sword; And their widows made no lamentation.

Then the Lord awaked as one asleep, Like a mighty man recovering from wine.

Tehillim- Book of Psalms

And He smote His adversaries backward; He put upon them a perpetual reproach.

Moreover, He abhorred the tent of Joseph, And chose not the tribe of Ephraim;

But chose the tribe of Judah, The mount Zion which He loved.

And He built His sanctuary like the heights, Like the earth which He hath founded for ever.

He chose David also His servant, And took him from the sheepfolds;

From following the ewes that give suck He brought him, To be shepherd over Jacob His people, and Israel His inheritance.

So he shepherded them according to the integrity of his heart; And lead them by the skilfulness of his hands.

Chapter 79

A Psalm of Asaph. O God, the heathen are come into Thine inheritance; They have defiled Thy holy temple; They have made Jerusalem into heaps.

They have given the dead bodies of Thy servants to be food unto the fowls of the heaven, The flesh of Thy saints unto the beasts of the earth.

They have shed their blood like water Round about Jerusalem, with none to bury them.

We are become a taunt to our neighbours, A scorn and derision to them that are round about us.

Tehillim- Book of Psalms

How long, O LORD, wilt Thou be angry for ever? How long will Thy jealousy burn like fire?

Pour out Thy wrath upon the nations that know Thee not, And upon the kingdoms that call not upon Thy name.

For they have devoured Jacob, And laid waste his habitation.

Remember not against us the iniquities of our forefathers; Let Thy compassions speedily come to meet us; For we are brought very low.

Help us, O God of our salvation, for the sake of the glory of Thy name; And deliver us, and forgive our sins, for Thy name's sake.

Wherefore should the nations say: 'Where is their God?' Let the avenging of Thy servants' blood that is shed Be made known among the nations in our sight..

Let the groaning of the prisoner come before Thee; According to the greatness of Thy power set free those that are appointed to death;

And render unto our neighbours sevenfold into their bosom Their reproach, wherewith they have reproached Thee, O Lord.

So we that are Thy people and the flock of Thy pasture Will give Thee thanks for ever; We will tell of Thy praise to all generations.

Chapter 80

For the Leader; upon Shoshannim. A testimony. A Psalm

Tehillim- Book of Psalms

of Asaph.

Give ear, O Shepherd of Israel, Thou that leadest Joseph like a flock; Thou that art enthroned upon the cherubim, shine forth.

Before Ephraim and Benjamin and Manasseh, stir up Thy might, And come to save us.

O God, restore us; And cause Thy face to shine, and we shall be saved.

O LORD God of hosts, How long wilt Thou be angry against the prayer of Thy people?

Thou hast fed them with the bread of tears, And given them tears to drink in large measure.

Thou makest us a strife unto our neighbours; And our enemies mock as they please.

O God of hosts, restore us; And cause Thy face to shine, and we shall be saved.

Thou didst pluck up a vine out of Egypt; Thou didst drive out the nations, and didst plant it.

Thou didst clear a place before it, And it took deep root, and filled the land.

The mountains were covered with the shadow of it, And the mighty cedars with the boughs thereof.

She sent out her branches unto the sea, And her shoots unto the River.

Why hast Thou broken down her fences, So that all they that pass by the way do pluck her?

The boar out of the wood doth ravage it, That which

Tehillim- Book of Psalms

moveth in the field feedeth on it.
O God of hosts, return, we beseech Thee; Look from heaven, and behold, and be mindful of this vine,
And of the stock which Thy right hand hath planted, And the branch that Thou madest strong for Thyself.
It is burned with fire; it is cut down; They perish at the rebuke of Thy countenance.
Let Thy hand be upon the man of Thy right hand, Upon the son of man whom Thou madest strong for Thyself.
So shall we not turn back from Thee; Quicken Thou us, and we will call upon Thy name.
O LORD God of hosts, restore us; Cause Thy face to shine, and we shall be saved.

Chapter 81
For the Leader; upon the Gittith. A Psalm of Asaph.
Sing aloud unto God our strength; shout unto the God of Jacob.
Take up the melody, and sound the timbrel, the sweet harp with the psaltery.
Blow the horn at the new moon, at the full moon for our feast-day.
For it is a statute for Israel, an ordinance of the God of Jacob.
He appointed it in Joseph for a testimony, when He went forth against the land of Egypt. The speech of one that I knew not did I hear:

Tehillim- Book of Psalms

'I removed his shoulder from the burden; His hands were freed from the basket.

Thou didst call in trouble, and I rescued thee; I answered thee in the secret place of thunder; I proved thee at the waters of Meribah. Selah

Hear, O My people, and I will admonish thee: O Israel, if thou wouldest hearken unto Me!

There shall no strange god be in thee; neither shalt thou worship any foreign god.

I am the LORD thy God, who brought thee up out of the land of Egypt; open thy mouth wide, and I will fill it.

But My people hearkened not to My voice; And Israel would none of Me.

So, I let them go after the stubbornness of their heart, That they might walk in their own counsels.

Oh, that My people would hearken unto Me, That Israel would walk in My ways!

I would soon subdue their enemies, And turn My hand against their adversaries.

The haters of the LORD should dwindle away before Him; And their punishment should endure for ever.

They should also be fed with the fat of wheat; and with honey out of the rock would I satisfy thee.'

Chapter 82

A Psalm of Asaph. God standeth in the congregation of God; in the midst of the judges He judgeth:

Tehillim- Book of Psalms

'How long will ye judge unjustly, and respect the persons of the wicked? Selah

Judge the poor and fatherless; do justice to the afflicted and destitute.

Rescue the poor and needy; deliver them out of the hand of the wicked.

They know not, neither do they understand; they go about in darkness; all the foundations of the earth are moved.

I said: Ye are godlike beings, and all of you sons of the Highest.

Nevertheless, ye shall die like men, and fall like one of the princes.'

Arise, O God, judge the earth; for Thou shalt possess all the nations.

Chapter 83

A Song, a Psalm of Asaph.

O God, keep not Thou silence; Hold not Thy peace, and be not still, O God.

For, lo, Thine enemies are in an uproar; And they that hate Thee have lifted up the head.

They hold crafty converse against Thy people, And take counsel against Thy treasured ones.

They have said: 'Come, and let us cut them off from being a nation; That the name of Israel may be no more in remembrance.'

For they have consulted together with one consent;

Tehillim- Book of Psalms

Against Thee do they make a covenant;
The tents of Edom and the Ishmaelites; Moab, and the Hagrites;
Gebal, and Ammon, and Amalek; Philistia with the inhabitants of Tyre;
Assyria also is joined with them; They have been an arm to the children of Lot. Selah
Do Thou unto them as unto Midian; As to Sisera, as to Jabin, at the brook Kishon;
Who were destroyed at En-dor; They became as dung for the earth.
Make their nobles like Oreb and Zeeb, And like Zebah and Zalmunna all their princes;
Who said: 'Let us take to ourselves in possession The habitations of God.'
O my God, make them like the whirling dust; As stubble before the wind.
As the fire that burneth the forest, And as the flame that setteth the mountains ablaze;
So pursue them with Thy tempest, And affright them with Thy storm.
Fill their faces with shame; That they may seek Thy name, O LORD.
Let them be ashamed and affrighted for ever; Yea, let them be abashed and perish;
That they may know that it is Thou alone whose name is the LORD, The Highest over all the earth.

Tehillim- Book of Psalms

Chapter 84

For the Leader; upon the Gittith. A Psalm of the sons of Korah.

How lovely are Thy tabernacles, O LORD of hosts!

My soul yearneth, yea, even pineth for the courts of the LORD; my heart and my flesh sing for joy unto the living God.

Yea, the sparrow hath found a house, and the swallow a nest for herself, Where she may lay her young; Thine altars, O LORD of hosts, My King, and my God -

Happy are they that dwell in Thy house, they are ever praising Thee. Selah

Happy is the man whose strength is in Thee; in whose heart are the highways.

Passing through the valley of Baca they make it a place of springs; yea, the early rain clotheth it with blessings.

They go from strength to strength, every one of them appeareth before God in Zion.

O LORD God of hosts, hear my prayer; give ear, O God of Jacob. Selah

Behold, O God our shield, and look upon the face of Thine anointed.

For a day in Thy courts is better than a thousand; I had rather stand at the threshold of the house of my God, than to dwell in the tents of wickedness.

For the LORD God is a sun and a shield; the LORD giveth grace and glory; No good thing will He withhold

Tehillim- Book of Psalms

from them that walk uprightly.

O LORD of hosts, happy is the man that trusteth in Thee.

Chapter 85

For the Leader. A Psalm of the sons of Korah.

LORD, Thou hast been favourable unto Thy land, Thou hast turned the captivity of Jacob.

Thou hast forgiven the iniquity of Thy people, Thou hast pardoned all their sin. Selah.

Thou hast withdrawn all Thy wrath; Thou hast turned from the fierceness of Thine anger.

Restore us, O God of our salvation, And cause Thine indignation toward us to cease.

Wilt Thou be angry with us for ever? Wilt Thou draw out Thine anger to all generations?

Wilt Thou not quicken us again, That Thy people may rejoice in Thee?

Show us Thy mercy, O LORD, And grant us Thy salvation.

I will hear what God the LORD will speak; For He will speak peace unto His people, and to His saints; But let them not turn back to folly.

Surely His salvation is nigh them that fear Him; That glory may dwell in our land.

Mercy and truth are met together; Righteousness and peace have kissed each other.

Truth springeth out of the earth; And righteousness hath

Tehillim- Book of Psalms

looked down from heaven.

Yea, the LORD will give that which is good; And our land shall yield her produce.

Righteousness shall go before Him, And shall make His footsteps a way.

Chapter 86

A Prayer of David. Incline Thine ear, O LORD, and answer me; For I am poor and needy.

Keep my soul, for I am godly; O Thou my God, save Thy servant that trusteth in Thee.

Be gracious unto me, O Lord; For unto Thee do I cry all the day.

Rejoice the soul of Thy servant; For unto Thee, O Lord, do I lift up my soul.

For Thou, Lord, art good, and ready to pardon, And plenteous in mercy unto all them that call upon Thee.

Give ear, O LORD, unto my prayer; And attend unto the voice of my supplications.

In the day of my trouble I call upon Thee; For Thou wilt answer me.

There is none like unto Thee among the gods, O Lord, And there are no works like Thine.

All nations whom Thou hast made shall come and prostrate themselves before Thee, O Lord; And they shall glorify Thy name.

For Thou art great, and doest wondrous things; Thou art

Tehillim- Book of Psalms

God alone.

Teach me, O LORD, Thy way, that I may walk in Thy truth; Make one my heart to fear Thy name.

I will thank Thee, O Lord my God, with my whole heart; And I will glorify Thy name for evermore.

For great is Thy mercy toward me; And Thou hast delivered my soul from the lowest nether-world.

O God, the proud are risen up against me, And the company of violent men have sought after my soul, And have not set Thee before them.

But Thou, O Lord, art a God full of compassion and gracious, Slow to anger, and plenteous in mercy and truth.

O turn unto me, and be gracious unto me; Give Thy strength unto Thy servant, And save the son of Thy handmaid.

Work in my behalf a sign for good; That they that hate me may see it, and be put to shame, Because Thou, LORD, hast helped me, and comforted me.

Chapter 87

A Psalm of the sons of Korah; a Song. His foundation is in the holy mountains.

The LORD loveth the gates of Zion more than all the dwellings of Jacob.

Glorious things are spoken of Thee, O city of God. Selah 'I will make mention of Rahab and Babylon as among

Tehillim- Book of Psalms

them that know Me; behold Philistia, and Tyre, with Ethiopia; this one was born there.'

But of Zion it shall be said: 'This man and that was born in her; And the Most High Himself doth establish her.'

The LORD shall count in the register of the peoples: 'This one was born there.' Selah

And whether they sing or dance, all my thoughts are in Thee.

Chapter 88

A Song, a Psalm of the sons of Korah; for the Leader; upon Mahalath Leannoth. Maschil of Heman the Ezrahite.

O LORD, God of my salvation, What time I cry in the night before Thee,

Let my prayer come before Thee, Incline Thine ear unto my cry.

For my soul is sated with troubles, And my life draweth nigh unto the grave.

I am counted with them that go down into the pit; I am become as a man that hath no help;

Set apart among the dead, Like the slain that lie in the grave, Whom Thou rememberest no more; And they are cut off from Thy hand.

Thou hast laid me in the nether-most pit, In dark places, in the deeps.

Thy wrath lieth hard upon me, And all Thy waves Thou pressest down. Selah

Tehillim- Book of Psalms

Thou hast put mine acquaintance far from me; Thou hast made me an abomination unto them; I am shut up, and I cannot come forth.

Mine eye languisheth by reason of affliction; I have called upon Thee, O LORD, every day, I have spread forth my hands unto Thee.

Wilt Thou work wonders for the dead? Or shall the shades arise and give Thee thanks? Selah

Shall Thy mercy be declared in the grave? Or Thy faithfulness in destruction?

Shall Thy wonders be known in the dark? And Thy righteousness in the land of forgetfulness?

But as for me, unto Thee, O LORD, do I cry, And in the morning doth my prayer come to meet Thee.

LORD, why castest Thou off my soul? Why hidest Thou Thy face from me?

I am afflicted and at the point of death from my youth up; I have borne Thy terrors, I am distracted.

Thy fierce wrath is gone over me; Thy terrors have cut me off.

They came round about me like water all the day; They compassed me about together.

Friend and companion hast Thou put far from me, And mine acquaintance into darkness.

Chapter 89

Maschil of Ethan the Ezrahite.

Tehillim- Book of Psalms

I will sing of the mercies of the LORD for ever; To all generations will I make known Thy faithfulness with my mouth.

For I have said: 'For ever is mercy built; In the very heavens Thou dost establish Thy faithfulness.

I have made a covenant with My chosen, I have sworn unto David My servant:

For ever will I establish thy seed, And build up thy throne to all generations.' Selah

So shall the heavens praise Thy wonders, O LORD, Thy faithfulness also in the assembly of the holy ones.

For who in the skies can be compared unto the LORD, Who among the sons of might can be likened unto the LORD,

A God dreaded in the great council of the holy ones, And feared of all them that are about Him?

O LORD God of hosts, Who is a mighty one, like unto Thee, O LORD? And Thy faithfulness is round about Thee.

Thou rulest the proud swelling of the sea; When the waves thereof arise, Thou stillest them.

Thou didst crush Rahab, as one that is slain; Thou didst scattered Thine enemies with the arm of Thy strength.

Thine are the heavens, Thine also the earth; The world and the fulness thereof, Thou hast founded them.

The north and the south, Thou hast created them; Tabor and Hermon rejoice in Thy name.

Tehillim- Book of Psalms

Thine is an arm with might; Strong is Thy hand, and exalted is Thy right hand.

Righteousness and justice are the foundation of Thy throne; Mercy and truth go before Thee.

Happy is the people that know the joyful shout; They walk, O LORD, in the light of Thy countenance.

In Thy name do they rejoice all the day; And through Thy righteousness are they exalted.

For Thou art the glory of their strength; And in Thy favour our horn is exalted.

For of the LORD is our shield; And the Holy One of Israel is our king.

Then Thou spokest in vision to Thy godly ones, And saidst: 'I have laid help upon one that is mighty; I have exalted one chosen out of the people.

I have found David My servant; With My holy oil have I anointed him;

With whom My hand shall be established; Mine arm also shall strengthen him.

The enemy shall not exact from him; Nor the son of wickedness afflict him.

And I will beat to pieces his adversaries before him, And smite them that hate him.

But My faithfulness and My mercy shall be with him; And through My name shall his horn be exalted.

I will set his hand also on the sea, And his right hand on the rivers.

Tehillim- Book of Psalms

He shall call unto Me: Thou art my Father, My God, and the rock of my salvation.

I also will appoint him first-born, The highest of the kings of the earth.

For ever will I keep for him My mercy, And My covenant shall stand fast with him.

His seed also will I make to endure for ever, And his throne as the days of heaven.

If his children forsake My law, And walk not in Mine ordinances; :

If they profane My statutes, And keep not My commandments;

Then will I visit their transgression with the rod, And their iniquity with strokes.

But My mercy will I not break off from him, Nor will I be false to My faithfulness.

My covenant will I not profane, Nor alter that which is gone out of My lips.

Once have I sworn by My holiness: Surely I will not be false unto David;

His seed shall endure for ever, And his throne as the sun before Me.

It shall be established for ever as the moon; And be stedfast as the witness in sky.' Selah

But Thou hast cast off and rejected, Thou hast been wroth with Thine anointed.

Thou hast abhorred the covenant of Thy servant; Thou

Tehillim- Book of Psalms

hast profaned his crown even to the ground.
Thou hast broken down all his fences; Thou hast brought his strongholds to ruin.
All that pass by the way spoil him; He is become a taunt to his neighbours.
Thou hast exalted the right hand of his adversaries; Thou hast made all his enemies to rejoice.
Yea, Thou turnest back the edge of his sword, And hast not made him to stand in the battle.
Thou hast made his brightness to cease, And cast his throne down to the ground.
The days of his youth hast Thou shortened; Thou hast covered him with shame. Selah
How long, O LORD, wilt Thou hide Thyself for ever? How long shall Thy wrath burn like fire?
O remember how short my time is; For what vanity hast Thou created all the children of men!
What man is he that liveth and shall not see death, That shall deliver his soul from the power of the grave? Selah
Where are Thy former mercies, O Lord, Which Thou didst swear unto David in Thy faithfulness?
Remember, Lord, the taunt of Thy servants; How I do bear in my bosom [the taunt of] so many peoples;
Wherewith Thine enemies have taunted, O LORD, Wherewith they have taunted the footsteps of Thine anointed.
Blessed be the LORD for evermore. Amen, and Amen.

Tehillim- Book of Psalms

Chapter 90

A Prayer of Moses the man of God. Lord, Thou hast been our dwelling-place in all generations.

Before the mountains were brought forth, Or ever Thou hadst formed the earth and the world, Even from everlasting to everlasting, Thou art God.

Thou turnest man to contrition; And sayest: 'Return, ye children of men.'

For a thousand years in Thy sight Are but as yesterday when it is past, And as a watch in the night.

Thou carriest them away as with a flood; they are as a sleep; In the morning they are like grass which groweth up.

In the morning it flourisheth, and groweth up; In the evening it is cut down, and withereth.

For we are consumed in Thine anger, And by Thy wrath are we hurried away.

Thou hast set our iniquities before Thee, Our secret sins in the light of Thy countenance.

For all our days are passed away in Thy wrath; We bring our years to an end as a tale that is told.

The days of our years are threescore years and ten, Or even by reason of strength fourscore years; Yet is their pride but travail and vanity; For it is speedily gone, and we fly away.

Who knoweth the power of Thine anger, And Thy wrath according to the fear that is due unto Thee?

Tehillim- Book of Psalms

So teach us to number our days, That we may get us a heart of wisdom.

Return, O LORD; how long? And let it repent Thee concerning Thy servants.

O satisfy us in the morning with Thy mercy; That we may rejoice and be glad all our days.

Make us glad according to the days wherein Thou hast afflicted us, according to the years wherein we have seen evil.

Let Thy work appears unto Thy servants, And Thy glory upon their children.

And let the graciousness of the Lord our God be upon us; Establish Thou also upon us the work of our hands; Yea, the work of our hands establishes Thou it.

Chapter 91

O thou that dwellest in the covert of the Most High, And abidest in the shadow of the Almighty;

I will say of the LORD, who is my refuge and my fortress, My God, in whom I trust,

That He will deliver thee from the snare of the fowler, And from the noisome pestilence.

He will cover thee with His pinions, And under His wings shalt thou take refuge; His truth is a shield and a buckler.

Thou shalt not be afraid of the terror by night, Nor of the arrow that flieth by day;

Of the pestilence that walketh in darkness, Nor of the

Tehillim- Book of Psalms

destruction that wasteth at noonday.

A thousand may fall at Thy side, And ten thousand at Thy right hand; It shall not come nigh thee.

Only with thine eyes shalt thou behold, And see the recompense of the wicked.

For thou hast made the LORD who is my refuge, Even the Most High, thy habitation.

There shall no evil befall thee, Neither shall any plague come nigh thy tent.

For He will give His angels charge over thee, To keep thee in all thy ways.

They shall bear thee upon their hands, Lest thou dash thy foot against a stone.

Thou shalt tread upon the lion and asp; The young lion and the serpent shalt thou trample under feet.

'Because he hath set his love upon Me, therefore will I deliver him; I will set him on high, because he hath known My name.

He shall call upon Me, and I will answer him; I will be with him in trouble; I will rescue him, and bring him to honour.

With long life will I satisfy him, And make Him to behold My salvation.

Chapter 92

A Psalm, a Song. For the sabbath day.

It is a good thing to give thanks unto the LORD, And to

Tehillim- Book of Psalms

sing praises unto Thy name, O Most High;
To declare Thy lovingkindness in the morning, And Thy faithfulness in the night seasons,
With an instrument of ten strings, and with the psaltery; With a solemn sound upon the harp.
For Thou, LORD, hast made me glad through Thy work; I will exult in the works of Thy hands.
How great are Thy works, O LORD! Thy thoughts are very deep.
A brutish man knoweth not, Neither doth a fool understand this.
When the wicked spring up as the grass, And when all the workers of iniquity do flourish; It is that they may be destroyed for ever.
But Thou, O LORD, art on high for evermore.
For, lo, Thine enemies, O LORD, For, lo, Thine enemies shall perish: All the workers of iniquity shall be scattered.
But my horn hast Thou exalted like the horn of the wild-ox; I am anointed with rich oil.
Mine eye also hath gazed on them that lie in wait for me, Mine ears have heard my desire of the evil-doers that rise up against me.
The righteous shall flourish like the palm-tree; He shall grow like a cedar in Lebanon.
Planted in the house of the LORD, They shall flourish in the courts of our God.
They shall still bring forth fruit in old age; They shall be

Tehillim- Book of Psalms

full of sap and richness;
To declare that the LORD is upright, My Rock, in whom there is no unrighteousness.

Chapter 93

The LORD reigneth; He is clothed in majesty; The LORD is clothed, He hath girded Himself with strength; Yea, the world is established, that it cannot be moved.
Thy throne is established of old; Thou art from everlasting.
The floods have lifted up, O LORD, The floods have lifted up their voice; The floods lift up their roaring.
Above the voices of many waters, The mighty breakers of the sea, The LORD on high is mighty.
Thy testimonies are very sure, Holiness becometh Thy house, O LORD, for evermore.

Chapter 94

O LORD, Thou God to whom vengeance belongeth, Thou God to whom vengeance belongeth, shine forth.
Lift up Thyself, Thou Judge of the earth; Render to the proud their recompense.
LORD, how long shall the wicked, How long shall the wicked exult?
They gush out, they speak arrogancy; All the workers of iniquity bear themselves loftily.
They crush Thy people, O LORD, And afflict Thy

Tehillim- Book of Psalms

heritage.

They slay the widow and the stranger, And murder the fatherless.

And they say: 'The LORD will not see, Neither will the God of Jacob give heed.'

Consider, ye brutish among the people; And ye fools, when will ye understand?

He that planted the ear, shall He not hear? He that formed the eye, shall He not see?

He that instructeth nations, shall not He correct? Even He that teacheth man knowledge?

The LORD knoweth the thoughts of man, That they are vanity.

Happy is the man whom Thou instructest, O LORD, And teachest out of Thy law;

That Thou mayest give him rest from the days of evil, Until the pit be digged for the wicked.

For the LORD will not cast off His people, Neither will He forsake His inheritance.

For right shall return unto justice, And all the upright in heart shall follow it.

Who will rise up for me against the evil-doers? Who will stand up for me against the workers of iniquity?

Unless the LORD had been my help, My soul had soon dwelt in silence.

If I say: 'My foot slippeth', Thy mercy, O LORD, holdeth me up.

Tehillim- Book of Psalms

When my cares are many within me, Thy comforts delight my soul.

Shall the seat of wickedness have fellowship with Thee, Which frameth mischief by statute?

They gather themselves together against the soul of the righteous, And condemn innocent blood.

But the LORD hath been my high tower, And my God the rock of my refuge.

And He hath brought upon them their own iniquity, And will cut them off in their own evil; The LORD our God will cut them off.

Chapter 95

O come, let us sing unto the LORD; Let us shout for joy to the Rock of our salvation.

Let us come before His presence with thanksgiving, Let us shout for joy unto Him with psalms.

For the LORD is a great God, And a great King above all gods;

In whose hand are the depths of the earth; The heights of the mountains are His also.

The sea is His, and He made it; And His hands formed the dry land.

O come, let us bow down and bend the knee; Let us kneel before the LORD our Maker;

For He is our God, And we are the people of His pasture, and the flock of His hand. To-day, if ye would but

Tehillim- Book of Psalms

hearken to His voice!

'Harden not your heart, as at Meribah, As in the day of Massah in the wilderness;

When your fathers tried Me, Proved Me, even though they saw My work.

For forty years was I wearied with that generation, And said: It is a people that do err in their heart, And they have not known My ways;

Wherefore I swore in My wrath, That they should not enter into My arest.'

Chapter 96

O sing unto the LORD a new song; Sing unto the LORD, all the earth.

Sing unto the LORD, bless His name; Proclaim His salvation from day to day.

Declare His glory among the nations, His marvellous works among all the peoples.

For great is the LORD, and highly to be praised; He is to be feared above all gods.

For all the gods of the peoples are things of nought; But the LORD made the heavens.

Honour and majesty are before Him; Strength and beauty are in His sanctuary.

Ascribe unto the LORD, ye kindreds of the peoples, Ascribe unto the LORD glory and strength.

Ascribe unto the LORD the glory due unto His name;

Tehillim- Book of Psalms

Bring an offering, and come into His courts.
O worship the LORD in the beauty of holiness; Tremble before Him, all the earth.
Say among the nations: 'The LORD reigneth.' The world also is established that it cannot be moved; He will judge the peoples with equity.
Let the heavens be glad, and let the earth rejoice; Let the sea roar, and the fulness thereof;
Let the field exult; and all that is therein; Then shall all the trees of the wood sing for joy;
Before the LORD, for He is come; For He is come to judge the earth; He will judge the world with righteousness, And the peoples in His faithfulness.

Chapter 97

The LORD reigneth; let the earth rejoice; Let the multitude of isles be glad.
Clouds and darkness are round about Him; Righteousness and justice are the foundation of His throne.
A fire goeth before Him, And burneth up His adversaries round about.
His lightnings lighted up the world; The earth saw, and trembled.
The mountains melted like wax at the presence of the LORD, At the presence of the Lord of the whole earth.
The heavens declared His righteousness, And all the peoples saw His glory.

Tehillim- Book of Psalms

Ashamed be all they that serve graven images, That boast themselves of things of nought; Bow down to Him, all ye gods.

Zion heard and was glad, And the daughters of Judah rejoiced; Because of Thy judgments, O LORD.

For Thou, LORD, art most high above all the earth; Thou art exalted far above all gods.

O ye that love the LORD, hate evil; He preserveth the souls of His saints; He delivered them out of the hand of the wicked.

Light is sown for the righteous, And gladness for the upright in heart.

Be glad in the LORD, ye righteous; And give thanks to His holy name.

Chapter 98

A Psalm. O sing unto the LORD a new song; For He hath done marvellous things; His right hand, and His holy arm, hath wrought salvation for Him.

The LORD hath made known His salvation; His righteousness hath He revealed in the sight of the nations.

He hath remembered His mercy and His faithfulness toward the house of Israel; All the ends of the earth have seen the salvation of our God.

Shout unto the LORD, all the earth; Break forth and sing for joy, yea, sing praises.

Sing praises unto the LORD with the harp; With the harp

Tehillim- Book of Psalms

and the voice of melody.

With trumpets and sound of the horn Shout ye before the King, the LORD.

Let the sea roar, and the fulness thereof; The world, and they that dwell therein;

Let the floods clap their hands; Let the mountains sing for joy together;

Before the LORD, for He is come to judge the earth; He will judge the world with righteousness, And the peoples with equity.

Chapter 99

The LORD reigneth; let the peoples tremble; He is enthroned upon the cherubim; let the earth quake.

The LORD is great in Zion; And He is high above all the peoples.

Let them praise Thy name as great and awful; Holy is He.

The strength also of the king who loveth justice— Thou hast established equity, Thou hast executed justice and righteousness in Jacob.

Exalt ye the LORD our God, And prostrate yourselves at His footstool; Holy is He.

Moses and Aaron among His priests, And Samuel among them that call upon His name, Did call upon the LORD, and He answered them.

He spoke unto them in the pillar of cloud; They kept His testimonies, and the statute that He gave them.

Tehillim- Book of Psalms

O LORD our God, Thou didst answer them; A forgiving God wast Thou unto them, Though Thou tookest vengeance of their misdeeds.

Exalt ye the LORD our God, And worship at His holy hill; For the LORD our God is holy.

Chapter 100

A Psalm of thanksgiving. Shout unto the LORD, all the earth.

Serve the LORD with gladness; come before His presence with singing.

Know ye that the LORD He is God; it is He that hath made us, and we are His, His people, and the flock of His pasture.

Enter into His gates with thanksgiving, and into His courts with praise; give thanks unto Him, and bless His name.

For the LORD is good; His mercy endureth for ever; and His faithfulness unto all generations.

Chapter 101

A Psalm of David. I will sing of mercy and justice; unto Thee, O LORD, will I sing praises.

I will give heed unto the way of integrity; oh when wilt Thou come unto me? I will walk within my house in the integrity of my heart.

I will set no base thing before mine eyes; I hate the doing

Tehillim- Book of Psalms

of things crooked; it shall not cleave unto me.

A perverse heart shall depart from me; I will know no evil thing.

Whoso slandereth his neighbour in secret, him will I destroy; Whoso is haughty of eye and proud of heart, him will I not suffer.

Mine eyes are upon the faithful of the land, that they may dwell with me; he that walketh in a way of integrity, he shall minister unto me.

He that worketh deceit shall not dwell within my house; he that speaketh falsehood shall not be established before mine eyes.

Morning by morning will I destroy all the wicked of the land; to cut off all the workers of iniquity from the city of the LORD.

Chapter 102

A Prayer of the afflicted, when he fainteth, and poureth out his complaint before the LORD.

O LORD, hear my prayer, and let my cry come unto Thee. Hide not Thy face from me in the day of my distress; incline Thine ear unto me; in the day when I call answer me speedily.

For my days are consumed like smoke, and my bones are burned as a hearth.

My heart is smitten like grass, and withered; for I forget to eat my bread.

Tehillim- Book of Psalms

By reason of the voice of my sighing My bones cleave to my flesh.

I am like a pelican of the wilderness; I am become as an owl of the waste places.

I watch, and am become like a sparrow that is alone upon the housetop.

Mine enemies taunt me all the day; they that are mad against me do curse by me.

For I have eaten ashes like bread, and mingled my drink with weeping,

Because of Thine indignation and Thy wrath; for Thou hast taken me up, and cast me away.

My days are like a lengthening shadow; and I am withered like grass.

But Thou, O LORD, sittest enthroned for ever; and Thy name is unto all generations.

Thou wilt arise, and have compassion upon Zion; for it is time to be gracious unto her, for the appointed time is come.

For Thy servants take pleasure in her stones, and love her dust.

So the nations will fear the name of the LORD, and all the kings of the earth Thy glory;

When the LORD hath built up Zion, when He hath appeared in His glory;

When He hath regarded the prayer of the destitute, And hath not despised their prayer.

Tehillim- Book of Psalms

This shall be written for the generation to come; And a people which shall be created shall praise the LORD.

For He hath looked down from the height of His sanctuary; From heaven did the LORD behold the earth;

To hear the groaning of the prisoner; To loose those that are appointed to death;

That men may tell of the name of the LORD in Zion, And His praise in Jerusalem;

When the peoples are gathered together, And the kingdoms, to serve the LORD.

He weakened my strength in the way; He shortened my days.

I say: 'O my God, take me not away in the midst of my days, Thou whose years endure throughout all generations.

Of old Thou didst lay the foundation of the earth; And the heavens are the work of Thy hands.

They shall perish, but Thou shalt endure; Yea, all of them shall wax old like a garment; As a vesture shalt Thou change them, and they shall pass away;

But Thou art the selfsame, And Thy years shall have no end.

The children of Thy servants shall dwell securely, And their seed shall be established before Thee.'

Chapter 103

A Psalm of David. Bless the LORD, O my soul; And all

Tehillim- Book of Psalms

that is within me, bless His holy name.

Bless the LORD, O my soul, And forget not all His benefits;

Who forgiveth all thine iniquity; Who healeth all Thy diseases;

Who redeemeth Thy life from the pit; Who encompasseth thee with lovingkindness and tender mercies;

Who satisfieth thine old age with good things; So that Thy youth is renewed like the eagle.

The LORD executeth righteousness, And acts of justice for all that are oppressed.

He made known His ways unto Moses, His doings unto the children of Israel.

The LORD is full of compassion and gracious, Slow to anger, and plenteous in mercy.

He will not always contend; Neither will He keep His anger for ever.

He hath not dealt with us after our sins, Nor requited us according to our iniquities.

For as the heaven is high above the earth, So great is His mercy toward them that fear Him.

As far as the east is from the west, So far hath He removed our transgressions from us.

Like as a father hath compassion upon his children, So hath the LORD compassion upon them that fear Him.

For He knoweth our frame; He remembereth that we are dust.

Tehillim- Book of Psalms

As for man, his days are as grass; As a flower of the field, so he flourisheth.

For the wind passeth over it, and it is gone; And the place thereof knoweth it no more.

But the mercy of the LORD is from everlasting to everlasting upon them that fear Him, And His righteousness unto children's children;

To such as keep His covenant, And to those that remember His precepts to do them.

The LORD hath established His throne in the heavens; And His kingdom ruleth over all.

Bless the LORD, ye angels of His, Ye mighty in strength, that fulfil His word, Hearkening unto the voice of His word.

Bless the LORD, all ye His hosts; Ye ministers of His, that do His pleasure.

Bless the LORD, all ye His works, In all places of His dominion; Bless the LORD, O my soul.

Chapter 104

Bless the LORD, O my soul. O LORD my God, Thou art very great; Thou art clothed with glory and majesty.

Who coverest Thyself with light as with a garment, who stretchest out the heavens like a curtain;

Who layest the beams of Thine upper chambers in the waters, who makest the clouds Thy chariot, who walkest upon the wings of the wind;

Tehillim- Book of Psalms

Who makest winds Thy messengers, the flaming fire Thy ministers.
Who didst establish the earth upon its foundations, that it should not be moved for ever and ever;
Thou didst cover it with the deep as with a vesture; the waters stood above the mountains.
At Thy rebuke they fled, at the voice of Thy thunder they hasted away—
The mountains rose, the valleys sank down— Unto the place which Thou hadst founded for them;
Thou didst set a bound which they should not pass over, That they might not return to cover the earth.
Who sendest forth springs into the valleys; They run between the mountains;
They give drink to every beast of the field, The wild asses quench their thirst.
Beside them dwell the fowl of the heaven, From among the branches they sing.
Who waterest the mountains from Thine upper chambers; The earth is full of the fruit of Thy works.
Who causeth the grass to spring up for the cattle, And herb for the service of man; To bring forth bread out of the earth,
And wine that maketh glad the heart of man, Making the face brighter than oil, And bread that stayeth man's heart.
The trees of the LORD have their fill, The cedars of Lebanon, which He hath planted;

Tehillim- Book of Psalms

Wherein the birds make their nests; As for the stork, the fir-trees are her house.

The high mountains are for the wild goats; The rocks are a refuge for the conies.

Who appointedst the moon for seasons; The sun knoweth his going down.

Thou makest darkness, and it is night, Wherein all the beasts of the forest do creep forth.

The young lions roar after their prey, And seek their food from God.

The sun ariseth, they slink away, And couch in their dens.

Man goeth forth unto his work And to his labour until the evening.

How manifold are Thy works, O LORD! In wisdom hast Thou made them all; The earth is full of Thy creatures.

Yonder sea, great and wide, Therein are creeping things innumerable, Living creatures, both small and great.

There go the ships; There is leviathan, whom Thou hast formed to sport therein.

All of them wait for Thee, That Thou mayest give them their food in due season.

Thou givest it unto them, they gather it; Thou openest Thy hand, they are satisfied with good.

Thou hidest Thy face, they vanish; Thou withdrawest their breath, they perish, And return to their dust.

Thou sendest forth Thy spirit, they are created; and Thou renewest the face of the earth.

Tehillim- Book of Psalms

May the glory of the LORD endure for ever; let the LORD rejoice in His works!

Who looketh on the earth, and it trembleth; He toucheth the mountains, and they smoke.

I will sing unto the LORD as long as I live; I will sing praise to my God while I have any being.

Let my musing be sweet unto Him; as for me, I will rejoice in the LORD.

Let sinners cease out of the earth, and let the wicked be no more. Bless the LORD, O my soul. Hallelujah.

Chapter 105

O give thanks unto the LORD, call upon His name; Make known His doings among the peoples.

Sing unto Him, sing praises unto Him; Speak ye of all His marvellous works.

Glory ye in His holy name; Let the heart of them rejoice that seek the LORD.

Seek ye the LORD and His strength; Seek His face continually.

Remember His marvellous works that He hath done, His wonders, and the judgments of His mouth;

O ye seed of Abraham His servant, Ye children of Jacob, His chosen ones.

He is the LORD our God; His judgments are in all the earth.

He hath remembered His covenant for ever, The word

Tehillim- Book of Psalms

which He commanded to a thousand generations;

The covenant which He made with Abraham, And His oath unto Isaac;

And He established it unto Jacob for a statute, To Israel for an everlasting covenant;

Saying: 'Unto thee will I give the land of Canaan, The lot of your inheritance.'

When they were but a few men in number. Yea, very few, and sojourners in it,

And when they went about from nation to nation, From one kingdom to another people,

He suffered no man to do them wrong, Yea, for their sake He reproved kings:

'Touch not Mine anointed ones, And do My prophets no harm.'

And He called a famine upon the land; He broke the whole staff of bread.

He sent a man before them; Joseph was sold for a servant; His feet they hurt with fetters, His person was laid in iron;

Until the time that his word came to pass, The word of the LORD tested him.

The king sent and loosed him; Even the ruler of the peoples, and set him free.

He made him lord of his house, And ruler of all his possessions;

To bind his princes at his pleasure, And teach his elders wisdom.

Tehillim- Book of Psalms

Israel also came into Egypt; And Jacob sojourned in the land of Ham.

And He increased His people greatly, And made them too mighty for their adversaries.

He turned their heart to hate His people, To deal craftily with His servants.

He sent Moses His servant, And Aaron whom He had chosen.

They wrought among them His manifold signs, And wonders in the land of Ham.

He sent darkness, and it was dark; And they rebelled not against His word.

He turned their waters into blood, And slew their fish.

Their land swarmed with frogs, In the chambers of their kings.

He spoke, and there came swarms of flies, And gnats in all their borders.

He gave them hail for rain, And flaming fire in their land.

He smote their vines also and their fig-trees; And broke the trees of their borders.

He spoke, and the locust came, And the canker-worm without number,

And did eat up every herb in their land, And did eat up the fruit of their ground.

He smote also all the first-born in their land, The first-fruits of all their strength.

And He brought them forth with silver and gold; And

Tehillim- Book of Psalms

there was none that stumbled among His tribes.

Egypt was glad when they departed; For the fear of them had fallen upon them.

He spread a cloud for a screen; And fire to give light in the night.

They asked, and He brought quails, And gave them in plenty the bread of heaven.

He opened the rock, and waters gushed out; They ran, a river in the dry places.

For He remembered His holy word Unto Abraham His servant;

And He brought forth His people with joy, His chosen ones with singing.

And He gave them the lands of the nations, And they took the labour of the peoples in possession;

That they might keep His statutes, And observe His laws. Hallelujah.

Chapter 106

Hallelujah. O give thanks unto the LORD; for He is good; for His mercy endureth for ever.

Who can express the mighty acts of the LORD, or make all His praise to be heard?

Happy are they that keep justice, that do righteousness at all times.

Remember me, O LORD, when Thou favourest Thy people; O think of me at Thy salvation;

Tehillim- Book of Psalms

That I may behold the prosperity of Thy chosen, that I may rejoice in the gladness of Thy nation, that I may glory with Thine inheritance.

We have sinned with our fathers, we have done iniquitously, we have dealt wickedly.

Our fathers in Egypt gave no heed unto Thy wonders; they remembered not the multitude of Thy mercies; but were rebellious at the sea, even at the Red Sea.

Nevertheless, He saved them for His name's sake, that He might make His mighty power to be known.

And He rebuked the Red Sea, and it was dried up; and He led them through the depths, as through a wilderness.

And He saved them from the hand of him that hated them, And redeemed them from the hand of the enemy.

And the waters covered their adversaries; There was not one of them left.

Then believed they His words; They sang His praise.

They soon forgot His works; They waited not for His counsel;

But lusted exceedingly in the wilderness, And tried God in the desert.

And He gave them their request; But sent leanness into their soul.

They were jealous also of Moses in the camp, And of Aaron the holy one of the LORD.

The earth opened and swallowed up Dathan, And covered the company of Abiram.

Tehillim- Book of Psalms

And a fire was kindled in their company; The flame burned up the wicked.

They made a calf in Horeb, And worshipped a molten image.

Thus, they exchanged their glory For the likeness of an ox that eateth grass.

They forgot God their saviour, Who had done great things in Egypt;

Wondrous works in the land of Ham, Terrible things by the Red Sea.

Therefore, He said that He would destroy them, Had not Moses His chosen stood before Him in the breach, To turn back His wrath, lest He should destroy them.

Moreover, they scorned the desirable land, They believed not His word;

And they murmured in their tents, They hearkened not unto the voice of the LORD.

Therefore, He swore concerning them, That He would overthrow them in the wilderness;

And that He would cast out their seed among the nations, And scatter them in the lands.

They joined themselves also unto Baal of Peor, And ate the sacrifices of the dead.

Thus, they provoked Him with their doings, And the plague broke in upon them.

Then stood up Phinehas, and wrought judgment, And so the plague was stayed.

Tehillim- Book of Psalms

And that was counted unto him for righteousness, Unto all generations for ever.

They angered Him also at the waters of Meribah, And it went ill with Moses because of them;

For they embittered his spirit, And he spoke rashly with his lips.

They did not destroy the peoples, As the LORD commanded them;

But mingled themselves with the nations, And learned their works;

And they served their idols, Which became a snare unto them;

Yea, they sacrificed their sons and their daughters unto demons,

And shed innocent blood, even the blood of their sons and of their daughters, Whom they sacrificed unto the idols of Canaan; And the land was polluted with blood.

Thus were they defiled with their works, And went astray in their doings.

Therefore, was the wrath of the LORD kindled against His people, And He abhorred His inheritance.

And He gave them into the hand of the nations; And they that hated them ruled over them.

Their enemies also oppressed them, And they were subdued under their hand.

Many times did He deliver them; But they were rebellious in their counsel, And sank low through their iniquity.

Tehillim- Book of Psalms

Nevertheless, He looked upon their distress, When He heard their cry;

And He remembered for them His covenant, And repented according to the multitude of His mercies.

He made them also to be pitied Of all those that carried them captive.

Save us, O LORD our God, And gather us from among the nations, That we may give thanks unto Thy holy name, That we may triumph in Thy praise.

Blessed be the LORD, the God of Israel, from everlasting even to everlasting, and let all the people say: 'Amen.' Hallelujah.

Chapter 107

'O give thanks unto the LORD, for He is good, For His mercy endureth for ever.'

So let the redeemed of the LORD say, Whom He hath redeemed from the hand of the adversary;

And gathered them out of the lands, From the east and from the west, From the north and from the sea.

They wandered in the wilderness in a desert way; They found no city of habitation.

Hungry and thirsty, Their soul fainted in them.

Then they cried unto the LORD in their trouble, And He delivered them out of their distresses.

And He led them by a straight way, That they might go to a city of habitation.

Tehillim- Book of Psalms

Let them give thanks unto the LORD for His mercy, And for His wonderful works to the children of men!

For He hath satisfied the longing soul, And the hungry soul He hath filled with good.

Such as sat in darkness and in the shadow of death, Being bound in affliction and iron—

Because they rebelled against the words of God, And contemned the counsel of the Most High.

Therefore, He humbled their heart with travail, They stumbled, and there was none to help—

They cried unto the LORD in their trouble, And He saved them out of their distresses.

He brought them out of darkness and the shadow of death, And broke their bands in sunder.

Let them give thanks unto the LORD for His mercy, And for His wonderful works to the children of men!

For He hath broken the gates of brass, And cut the bars of iron in sunder.

Crazed because of the way of their transgression, And afflicted because of their iniquities—

Their soul abhorred all manner of food, And they drew near unto the gates of death—

They cried unto the LORD in their trouble, And He saved them out of their distresses;

He sent His word, and healed them, And delivered them from their graves.

Tehillim- Book of Psalms

Let them give thanks unto the LORD for His mercy, And for His wonderful works to the children of men!

And let them offer the sacrifices of thanksgiving, And declare His works with singing.

They that go down to the sea in ships, That do business in great waters—

These saw the works of the LORD, And His wonders in the deep;

For He commanded, and raised the stormy wind, Which lifted up the waves thereof;

They mounted up to the heaven, they went down to the deeps; Their soul melted away because of trouble;

They reeled to and fro, and staggered like a drunken man, And all their wisdom was swallowed up -

They cried unto the LORD in their trouble, And He brought them out of their distresses.

He made the storm a calm, So that the waves thereof were still.

Then were they glad because they were quiet, And He led them unto their desired haven.

Let them give thanks unto the LORD for His mercy, And for His wonderful works to the children of men!

Let them exalt Him also in the assembly of the people, And praise Him in the seat of the elders.

He turneth rivers into a wilderness, And watersprings into a thirsty ground;

A fruitful land into a salt waste, For the wickedness of

Tehillim- Book of Psalms

them that dwell therein.

He turneth a wilderness into a pool of water, And a dry land into watersprings.

And there He maketh the hungry to dwell, And they establish a city of habitation;

And sow fields, and plant vineyards, Which yield fruits of increase.

He blesseth them also, so that they are multiplied greatly, And suffereth not their cattle to decrease.

Again, they are minished and dwindle away Through oppression of evil and sorrow.

He poureth contempt upon princes, And causeth them to wander in the waste, where there is no way.

Yet setteth He the needy on high from affliction, And maketh his families like a flock.

The upright see it, and are glad; And all iniquity stoppeth her mouth.

Whoso is wise, let him observe these things, And let them consider the mercies of the LORD.

Chapter 108

A Song, a Psalm of David.

My heart is steadfast, O God; I will sing, yea, I will sing praises, even with my glory.

Awake, psaltery and harp; I will awake the dawn.

I will give thanks unto Thee, O LORD, among the peoples; And I will sing praises unto Thee among the

Tehillim- Book of Psalms

nations.

For Thy mercy is great above the heavens, And Thy truth reacheth unto the skies.

Be Thou exalted, O God, above the heavens; And Thy glory be above all the earth.

That Thy beloved may be delivered, Save with Thy right hand, and answer me.

God spoke in His holiness, that I would exult; That I would divide Shechem, and mete out the valley of Succoth.

Gilead is mine, Manasseh is mine; Ephraim also is the defence of my head; Judah is my sceptre.

Moab is my washpot; Upon Edom do I cast my shoe; Over Philistia do I cry aloud.

Who will bring me into the fortified city? Who will lead me unto Edom?

Hast not Thou cast us off, O God? And Thou goest not forth, O God, with our hosts?

Give us help against the adversary; For vain is the help of man.

Through God we shall do valiantly; For He it is that will tread down our adversaries.

Chapter 109

For the Leader. A Psalm of David. O God of my praise, keep not silence;

For the mouth of the wicked and the mouth of deceit have

Tehillim- Book of Psalms

they opened against me; They have spoken unto me with a lying tongue.

They compassed me about also with words of hatred, And fought against me without a cause.

In return for my love they are my adversaries; But I am all prayer.

And they have laid upon me evil for good, And hatred for my love:

'Set Thou a wicked man over him; And let an adversary stand at his right hand.

When he is judged, let him go forth condemned; And let his prayer be turned into sin.

Let his days be few; Let another take his charge.

Let his children be fatherless, And his wife a widow.

Let his children be vagabonds, and beg; And let them seek their bread out of their desolate places.

Let the creditor distrain all that he hath; And let strangers make spoil of his labour.

Let there be none to extend kindness unto him; Neither let there be any to be gracious unto his fatherless children.

Let his posterity be cut off; In the generation following let their name be blotted out.

Let the iniquity of his fathers be brought to remembrance unto the LORD; And let not the sin of his mother be blotted out.

Let them be before the LORD continually, That He may cut off the memory of them from the earth.

Tehillim- Book of Psalms

Because that he remembered not to do kindness, But persecuted the poor and needy man, And the broken in heart he was ready to slay.

Yea, he loved cursing, and it came unto him; And he delighted not in blessing, and it is far from him.

He clothed himself also with cursing as with his raiment, And it is come into his inward parts like water, And like oil into his bones.

Let it be unto him as the garment which he putteth on, And for the girdle wherewith he is girded continually.'

This would mine adversary's effect from the LORD, And they that speak evil against my soul.

But Thou, O GOD the Lord, deal with me for Thy name's sake; Because Thy mercy is good, deliver Thou me.

For I am poor and needy, And my heart is wounded within me.

I am gone like the shadow when it lengtheneth; I am shaken off as the locust.

My knees totter through fasting; And my flesh is lean, and hath no fatness.

I am become also a taunt unto them; When they see me, they shake their head.

Help me, O LORD my God; O save me according to Thy mercy;

That they may know that this is Thy hand; That Thou, LORD, hast done it.

Let them curse, but bless Thou; When they arise, they

Tehillim- Book of Psalms

shall be put to shame, but Thy servant shall rejoice.

Mine adversaries shall be clothed with confusion, And shall put on their own shame as a robe.

I will give great thanks unto the LORD with my mouth; Yea, I will praise Him among the multitude;

Because He standeth at the right hand of the needy, To save him from them that judge his soul.

Chapter 110

A Psalm of David. The LORD saith unto my lord: 'Sit thou at My right hand, until I make thine enemies thy footstool.'

The rod of Thy strength the LORD will send out of Zion: 'Rule thou in the midst of thine enemies.'

Thy people offer themselves willingly in the day of thy warfare; in adornments of holiness, from the womb of the dawn, Thine is the dew of thy youth.

The LORD hath sworn, and will not repent: 'Thou art a priest for ever After the manner of Melchizedek.'

The Lord at thy right hand Doth crush kings in the day of His wrath.

He will judge among the nations; He filleth it with the dead bodies, He crusheth the head over a wide land.

He will drink of the brook in the way; Therefore will he lift up the head.

Chapter 111

Hallelujah. I will give thanks unto the LORD with my

Tehillim- Book of Psalms

whole heart, In the council of the upright, and in the congregation.
The works of the LORD are great, Sought out of all them that have delight therein.
His work is glory and majesty; And His righteousness endureth for ever.
He hath made a memorial for His wonderful works; The LORD is gracious and full of compassion.
He hath given food unto them that fear Him; He will ever be mindful of His covenant.
He hath declared to His people the power of His works, In giving them the heritage of the nations.
The works of His hands are truth and justice; All His precepts are sure.
They are established for ever and ever, They are done in truth and uprightness.
He hath sent redemption unto His people; He hath commanded His covenant for ever; Holy and awful is His name.
The fear of the LORD is the beginning of wisdom; A good understanding have all they that do thereafter; His praise endureth for ever.

Chapter 112

Hallelujah. Happy is the man that feareth the LORD, That delighteth greatly in His commandments.
His seed shall be mighty upon earth; The generation of

Tehillim- Book of Psalms

the upright shall be blessed.

Wealth and riches are in his house; And his merit endureth for ever.

Unto the upright He shineth as a light in the darkness, Gracious, and full of compassion, and righteous.

Well is it with the man that dealeth graciously and lendeth, That ordereth his affairs rightfully.

For he shall never be moved; The righteous shall be had in everlasting remembrance.

He shall not be afraid of evil tidings; His heart is stedfast, trusting in the LORD.

His heart is established, he shall not be afraid, Until he gaze upon his adversaries.

He hath scattered abroad, he hath given to the needy; His righteousness endureth for ever; His horn shall be exalted in honour.

The wicked shall see it, and be vexed; he shall gnash with his teeth, and melt away; the desire of the wicked shall perish.

Chapter 113

Hallelujah. Praise, O ye servants of the LORD, Praise the name of the LORD.

Blessed be the name of the LORD From this time forth and for ever.

From the rising of the sun unto the going down thereof The LORD'S name is to be praised.

Tehillim- Book of Psalms

The LORD is high above all nations, His glory is above the heavens.
Who is like unto the LORD our God, That is enthroned on high,
That looketh down low Upon heaven and upon the earth?
Who raiseth up the poor out of the dust, And lifteth up the needy out of the dunghill;
That He may set him with princes, Even with the princes of His people.
Who maketh the barren woman to dwell in her house As a joyful mother of children. Hallelujah.

Chapter 114

When Israel came forth out of Egypt, The house of Jacob from a people of strange language;
Judah became His sanctuary, Israel His dominion.
The sea saw it, and fled; The Jordan turned backward.
The mountains skipped like rams, The hills like young sheep.
What aileth thee, O thou sea, that thou fleest? Thou Jordan, that thou turnest backward?
Ye mountains, that ye skip like rams; Ye hills, like young sheep?
Tremble, thou earth, at the presence of the Lord, At the presence of the God of Jacob;
Who turned the rock into a pool of water, The flint into a fountain of waters.

Tehillim- Book of Psalms

Chapter 115

Not unto us, O LORD, not unto us, But unto Thy name give glory, For Thy mercy, and for Thy truth's sake.

Wherefore should the nations say: 'Where is now their God?'

But our God is in the heavens; Whatsoever pleased Him He hath done.

Their idols are silver and gold, The work of men's hands.

They have mouths, but they speak not; Eyes have they, but they see not;

They have ears, but they hear not; Noses have they, but they smell not;

They have hands, but they handle not; Feet have they, but they walk not; Neither speak they with their throat.

They that make them shall be like unto them; Yea, every one that trusteth in them.

O Israel, trust thou in the LORD! He is their help and their shield!

O house of Aaron, trust ye in the LORD! He is their help and their shield!

Ye that fear the LORD, trust in the LORD! He is their help and their shield.

The LORD hath been mindful of us, He will bless— He will bless the house of Israel; He will bless the house of Aaron.

He will bless them that fear the LORD, Both small and great.

Tehillim- Book of Psalms

The LORD increase you more and more, You and your children.
Blessed be ye of the LORD Who made heaven and earth.
The heavens are the heavens of the LORD; But the earth hath He given to the children of men.
The dead praise not the LORD, Neither any that go down into silence;
But we will bless the LORD From this time forth and for ever. Hallelujah.

Chapter 116
I love that the LORD should hear my voice and my supplications.
Because He hath inclined His ear unto me, therefore will I call upon Him all my days.
The cords of death compassed me, And the straits of the nether-world got hold upon me; I found trouble and sorrow.
But I called upon the name of the LORD: 'I beseech thee, O LORD, deliver my soul.'
Gracious is the LORD, and righteous; Yea, our God is compassionate.
The LORD preserveth the simple; I was brought low, and He saved me.
Return, O my soul, unto Thy rest; For the LORD hath dealt bountifully with thee.
For thou hast delivered my soul from death, Mine eyes

Tehillim - Book of Psalms

from tears, And my feet from stumbling.
I shall walk before the LORD In the lands of the living.
I trusted even when I spoke: 'I am greatly afflicted.'
I said in my haste: 'All men are liars.'
How can I repay unto the LORD All His bountiful dealings toward me?
I will lift up the cup of salvation, And call upon the name of the LORD.
My vows will I pay unto the LORD, Yea, in the presence of all His people.
Precious in the sight of the LORD Is the death of His saints.
I beseech Thee, O LORD, for I am Thy servant; I am Thy servant, the son of Thy handmaid; Thou hast loosed my bands.
I will offer to thee the sacrifice of thanksgiving, And will call upon the name of the LORD.
I will pay my vows unto the LORD, Yea, in the presence of all His people;
In the courts of the LORD'S house, In the midst of thee, O Jerusalem. Hallelujah.

Chapter 117

O praise the LORD, all ye nations; Laud Him, all ye peoples.
For His mercy is great toward us; And the truth of the LORD endureth for ever. Hallelujah.

Tehillim- Book of Psalms

Chapter 118
'O give thanks unto the LORD, for He is good, For His mercy endureth for ever.
So let Israel now say, For His mercy endureth for ever,
So let the house of Aaron now say, For His mercy endureth for ever.
So let them now that fear the LORD say, For His mercy endureth for ever.
Out of my straits I called upon the LORD; He answered me with great enlargement.
The LORD is for me; I will not fear; What can man do unto me?
The LORD is for me as my helper; And I shall gaze upon them that hate me.
It is better to take refuge in the LORD Than to trust in man.
It is better to take refuge in the LORD Than to trust in princes.
All nations compass me about; Verily, in the name of the LORD I will cut them off.
They compass me about, yea, they compass me about; Verily, in the name of the LORD I will cut them off.
They compass me about like bees; They are quenched as the fire of thorns; Verily, in the name of the LORD I will cut them off.
Thou didst thrust sore at me that I might fall; But the LORD helped me.

Tehillim- Book of Psalms

The LORD is my strength and song; And He is become my salvation.

The voice of rejoicing and salvation is in the tents of the righteous; The right hand of the LORD doeth valiantly.

The right hand of the LORD is exalted; The right hand of the LORD doeth valiantly.

I shall not die, but live, And declare the works of the LORD.

The LORD hath chastened me sore; But He hath not given me over unto death.

Open to me the gates of righteousness; I will enter into them, I will give thanks unto the LORD.

This is the gate of the LORD; The righteous shall enter into it.

I will give thanks unto Thee, for Thou hast answered me, And art become my salvation.

The stone which the builders rejected Is become the chief corner-stone.

This is the LORD'S doing; It is marvellous in our eyes.

This is the day which the LORD hath made; We will rejoice and be glad in it.

We beseech Thee, O LORD, save now! We beseech Thee, O LORD, make us now to prosper!

Blessed be he that cometh in the name of the LORD; We bless you out of the house of the LORD.

The LORD is God, and hath given us light; Order the festival procession with boughs, even unto the horns of

Tehillim- Book of Psalms

the altar.

Thou art my God, and I will give thanks unto Thee; Thou art my God, I will exalt Thee.

O give thanks unto the LORD, for He is good, For His mercy endureth for ever.

Chapter 119
ALEPH.

Happy are they that are upright in the way, who walk in the law of the LORD.

Happy are they that keep His testimonies, that seek Him with the whole heart.

Yea, they do no unrighteousness; they walk in His ways.

Thou hast ordained Thy precepts, that we should observe them diligently.

Oh that my ways were directed to observe Thy statutes!

Then should I not be ashamed, when I have regard unto all Thy commandments.

I will give thanks unto Thee with uprightness of heart, when I learn Thy righteous ordinances.

I will observe Thy statutes; O forsake me not utterly.

BETH.

Wherewithal shall a young man keep his way pure? By taking heed thereto according to Thy word.

With my whole heart have I sought Thee; O let me not err from Thy commandments.

Tehillim- Book of Psalms

Thy word have I laid up in my heart, that I might not sin against Thee.
Blessed art Thou, O LORD; Teach me Thy statutes.
With my lips have I told All the ordinances of Thy mouth.
I have rejoiced in the way of Thy testimonies, As much as in all riches.
I will meditate in Thy precepts, And have respect unto Thy ways.
I will delight myself in Thy statutes; I will not forget Thy word.

GIMEL.
Deal bountifully with Thy servant that I may live, and I will observe Thy word.
Open Thou mine eyes, that I may behold wondrous things out of Thy law.
I am a sojourner in the earth; hide not Thy commandments from me.
My soul breaketh for the longing that it hath unto Thine ordinances at all times.
Thou hast rebuked the proud that are cursed, that do err from Thy commandments.
Take away from me reproach and contempt; for I have kept Thy testimonies.
Even though princes sit and talk against me, Thy servant doth meditate in Thy statutes.

Tehillim- Book of Psalms

Yea, Thy testimonies are my delight, they are my counsellors.

DALETH.
My soul cleaveth unto the dust; quicken Thou me according to Thy word.
I told of my ways, and Thou didst answer me; teach me Thy statutes.
Make me to understand the way of Thy precepts, that I may talk of Thy wondrous works.
My soul melteth away for heaviness; sustain me according unto Thy word.
Remove from me the way of falsehood; and grant me Thy law graciously.
I have chosen the way of faithfulness; Thine ordinances have I set [before me].
I cleave unto Thy testimonies; O LORD, put me not to shame.
I will run the way of Thy commandments, For Thou dost enlarge my heart.

HE.
Teach me, O LORD, the way of Thy statutes; And I will keep it at every step.
Give me understanding, that I keep Thy law and observe it with my whole heart.
Make me to tread in the path of Thy commandments; for

Tehillim- Book of Psalms

therein do I delight.

Incline my heart unto Thy testimonies, and not to covetousness.

Turn away mine eyes from beholding vanity, and quicken me in Thy ways.

Confirm Thy word unto Thy servant, which pertaineth unto the fear of Thee.

Turn away my reproach which I dread; for Thine ordinances are good.

Behold, I have longed after Thy precepts; quicken me in Thy righteousness.

VAV.

Let Thy mercies also come unto me, O LORD, even Thy salvation, according to Thy word;

That I may have an answer for him that taunteth me; for I trust in Thy word.

And take not the word of truth utterly out of my mouth; for I hope in Thine ordinances;

So shall I observe Thy law continually for ever and ever;

And I will walk at ease, for I have sought Thy precepts;

I will also speak of Thy testimonies before kings, and will not be ashamed.

And I will delight myself in Thy commandments, which I have loved.

I will lift up my hands also unto Thy commandments, which I have loved; And I will meditate in Thy statutes.

Tehillim- Book of Psalms

ZAIN.

Remember the word unto Thy servant, Because Thou hast made me to hope.

This is my comfort in my affliction, that Thy word hath quickened me.

The proud have had me greatly in derision; yet have I not turned aside from Thy law.

I have remembered Thine ordinances which are of old, O LORD, and have comforted myself.

Burning indignation hath taken hold upon me, because of the wicked that forsake Thy law.

Thy statutes have been my songs in the house of my pilgrimage.

I have remembered Thy name, O LORD, in the night, and have observed Thy law.

This I have had, that I have kept Thy precepts.

HETH.

My portion is the LORD, I have said that I would observe Thy words.

I have entreated Thy favour with my whole heart; be gracious unto me according to Thy word.

I considered my ways, and turned my feet unto Thy testimonies.

I made haste, and delayed not, to observe Thy commandments.

The bands of the wicked have enclosed me; but I have not

Tehillim- Book of Psalms

forgotten Thy law.

At midnight I will rise to give thanks unto Thee because of Thy righteous ordinances.

I am a companion of all them that fear Thee, and of them that observe Thy precepts.

The earth, O LORD, is full of Thy mercy; teach me Thy statutes.

TETH.

Thou hast dealt well with Thy servant, O LORD, according unto Thy word.

Teach me good discernment and knowledge; for I have believed in Thy commandments.

Before I was afflicted, I did err; But now I observe Thy word.

Thou art good, and doest good; Teach me Thy statutes.

The proud have forged a lie against me; But I with my whole heart will keep Thy precepts.

Their heart is gross like fat; But I delight in Thy law.

It is good for me that I have been afflicted, In order that I might learn Thy statutes.

The law of Thy mouth is better unto me Than thousands of gold and silver.

JOD.

Thy hands have made me and fashioned me; Give me understanding, that I may learn Thy commandments.

Tehillim- Book of Psalms

They that fear Thee shall see me and be glad, because I have hope in Thy word.
I know, O LORD, that Thy judgments are righteous, and that in faithfulness Thou hast afflicted me.
Let, I pray Thee, Thy lovingkindness be ready to comfort me, According to Thy promise unto Thy servant.
Let Thy tender mercies come unto me, that I may live; for Thy law is my delight.
Let the proud be put to shame, for they have distorted my cause with falsehood; but I will meditate in Thy precepts.
Let those that fear Thee return unto me, and they that know Thy testimonies.
Let my heart be undivided in Thy statutes, in order that I may not be put to shame.

CAPH.
My soul pineth for Thy salvation; in Thy word do I hope.
Mine eyes fail for Thy word, Saying: 'When wilt Thou comfort me?'
For I am become like a wine-skin in the smoke; yet do I not forget Thy statutes.
How many are the days of Thy servant? When wilt Thou execute judgment on them that persecute me?
The proud have digged pits for me, which is not according to Thy law.
All Thy commandments are faithful; they persecute me for nought; help Thou me.

Tehillim- Book of Psalms

They had almost consumed me upon earth; but as for me, I forsook not Thy precepts.
Quicken me after Thy lovingkindness, and I will observe the testimony of Thy mouth.

LAMED.
For ever, O LORD, Thy word standeth fast in heaven.
Thy faithfulness is unto all generations; Thou hast established the earth, and it standeth.
They stand this day according to Thine ordinances; for all things are Thy servants.
Unless Thy law had been my delight, I should then have perished in mine affliction.
I will never forget Thy precepts; for with them Thou hast quickened me.
I am Thine, save me; for I have sought Thy precepts.
The wicked have waited for me to destroy me; but I will consider Thy testimonies.
I have seen an end to every purpose; but Thy commandment is exceeding broad.

MEM.
O how love I Thy law! It is my meditation all the day.
Thy commandments make me wiser than mine enemies: For they are ever with me.
I have more understanding than all my teachers; For Thy testimonies are my meditation.

Tehillim- Book of Psalms

I understand more than mine elders, because I have keep Thy precepts.
I have refrained my feet from every evil way, in order that I might observe Thy word.
I have not turned aside from Thine ordinances; For Thou hast instructed me.
How sweet are Thy words unto my palate! Yea, sweeter than honey to my mouth!
From Thy precepts I get understanding; Therefore, I hate every false way.

NUN.
Thy word is a lamp unto my feet, And a light unto my path.
I have sworn, and have confirmed it, To observe Thy righteous ordinances.
I am afflicted very much; Quicken me, O LORD, according unto Thy word.
Accept, I beseech Thee, the freewill-offerings of my mouth, O LORD, And teach me Thine ordinances.
My soul is continually in my hand; yet have I not forgotten Thy law.
The wicked have laid a snare for me; yet went I not astray from Thy precepts.
Thy testimonies have I taken as a heritage for ever; for they are the rejoicing of my heart.
I have inclined my heart to perform Thy statutes, for ever,

Tehillim- Book of Psalms

at every step.

SAMECH.
I hate them that are of a double mind; but Thy law do I love.
Thou art my covert and my shield; in Thy word do I hope.
Depart from me, ye evildoers; that I may keep the commandments of my God.
Uphold me according unto Thy word, that I may live; and put me not to shame in my hope.
Support Thou me, and I shall be saved; and I will occupy myself with Thy statutes continually.
Thou hast made light of all them that err from Thy statutes; for their deceit is vain.
Thou puttest away all the wicked of the earth like dross; therefore, I love Thy testimonies.
My flesh shuddereth for fear of Thee; And I am afraid of Thy judgments.

AIN.
I have done justice and righteousness; Leave me not to mine oppressors.
Be surety for Thy servant for good; Let not the proud oppress me.
Mine eyes fail for Thy salvation, and for Thy righteous word.
Deal with Thy servant according unto Thy mercy, and

Tehillim- Book of Psalms

teach me Thy statutes.
I am Thy servant, give me understanding, that I may know Thy testimonies.
It is time for the LORD to work; They have made void Thy law.
Therefore, I love Thy commandments Above gold, yea, above fine gold.
Therefore, I esteem all [Thy] precepts concerning all things to be right; Every false way I hate.

PE.
Thy testimonies are wonderful; Therefore, doth my soul keep them.
The opening of Thy words giveth light; it giveth understanding unto the simple.
I opened wide my mouth, and panted; For I longed for Thy commandments.
Turn Thee towards me, and be gracious unto me, As is Thy wont to do unto those that love Thy name.
Order my footsteps by Thy word; And let not any iniquity have dominion over me.
Redeem me from the oppression of man, And I will observe Thy precepts.
Make Thy face to shine upon Thy servant; And teach me Thy statutes.
Mine eyes run down with rivers of water, Because they observe not Thy law.

Tehillim- Book of Psalms

TZADE.

Righteous art Thou, O LORD, And upright are Thy judgments.

Thou hast commanded Thy testimonies in righteousness and exceeding faithfulness.

My zeal hath undone me, because mine adversaries have forgotten Thy words.

Thy word is tried to the uttermost, and Thy servant loveth it.

I am small and despised; yet have I not forgotten Thy precepts.

Thy righteousness is an everlasting righteousness, and Thy law is truth.

Trouble and anguish have overtaken me; yet Thy commandments are my delight.

Thy testimonies are righteous for ever; give me understanding, and I shall live.

KOPH.

I have called with my whole heart; answer me, O LORD; I will keep Thy statutes.

I have called Thee, save me, and I will observe Thy testimonies.

I rose early at dawn, and cried; I hoped in Thy word.

Mine eyes forestalled the night-watches, that I might meditate in Thy word.

Hear my voice according unto Thy lovingkindness;

Tehillim- Book of Psalms

Quicken me, O LORD, as Thou art wont.
They draw nigh that follow after wickedness; they are far from Thy law.
Thou art nigh, O LORD; and all Thy commandments are truth.
Of old have I known from Thy testimonies that Thou hast founded them for ever.

RESH.
O see mine affliction, and rescue me; For I do not forget Thy law.
Plead Thou my cause, and redeem me; Quicken me according to Thy word.
Salvation is far from the wicked; For they seek not Thy statutes.
Great are Thy compassions, O LORD; Quicken me as Thou art wont.
Many are my persecutors and mine adversaries; Yet have I not turned aside from Thy testimonies.
I beheld them that were faithless, and strove with them; Because they observed not Thy word.
O see how I love Thy precepts; Quicken me, O LORD, according to Thy lovingkindness.
The beginning of Thy word is truth; And all Thy righteous ordinance endureth for ever.

Tehillim- Book of Psalms

SCHIN.

Princes have persecuted me without a cause; But my heart standeth in awe of Thy words.

I rejoice at Thy word, As one that findeth great spoil.

I hate and abhor falsehood; Thy law do I love..

Seven times a day do I praise Thee, because of Thy righteous ordinances.

Great peace have they that love Thy law; And there is no stumbling for them.

I have hoped for Thy salvation, O LORD, And have done Thy commandments.

My soul hath observed Thy testimonies; And I love them exceedingly.

I have observed Thy precepts and Thy testimonies; For all my ways are before Thee.

TAV.

Let my cry come near before Thee, O LORD; Give me understanding according to Thy word.

Let my supplication come before Thee; deliver me according to Thy word.

Let my lips utter praise: Because Thou teachest me Thy statutes.

Let my tongue sing of Thy word; For all Thy commandments are righteousness.

Let Thy hand be ready to help me; For I have chosen Thy precepts.

Tehillim- Book of Psalms

I have longed for Thy salvation, O LORD; And Thy law is my delight.

Let my soul live, and it shall praise Thee; And let Thine ordinances help me.

I have gone astray like a lost sheep; seek Thy servant; For I have not forgotten Thy commandments.

Chapter 120

A Song of Ascents. In my distress I called unto the LORD, And He answered me.

O LORD, deliver my soul from lying lips, From a deceitful tongue.

What shall be given unto thee, and what shall be done more unto thee, Thou deceitful tongue?

Sharp arrows of the mighty, With coals of broom.

Woe is me, that I sojourn with Meshech, That I dwell beside the tents of Kedar!

My soul hath full long had her dwelling With him that hateth peace.

I am all peace; But when I speak, they are for war.

Chapter 121

A Song of Ascents. I will lift up mine eyes unto the mountains: From whence shall my help come?

My help cometh from the LORD, Who made heaven and earth.

He will not suffer thy foot to be moved; He that keepeth

Tehillim- Book of Psalms

thee will not slumber.

Behold, He that keepeth Israel Doth neither slumber nor sleep.

The LORD is thy keeper; The LORD is thy shade upon thy right hand.

The sun shall not smite thee by day, Nor the moon by night.

The LORD shall keep thee from all evil; He shall keep thy soul.

The LORD shall guard thy going out and thy coming in, From this time forth and for ever.

Chapter 122

A Song of Ascents; of David. I rejoiced when they said unto me: 'Let us go unto the house of the LORD.'

Our feet are standing within thy gates, O Jerusalem;

Jerusalem, that art builded as a city that is compact together;

Whither the tribes went up, even the tribes of the LORD, as a testimony unto Israel, to give thanks unto the name of the LORD.

For there were set thrones for judgment, the thrones of the house of David.

Pray for the peace of Jerusalem; May they prosper that love thee.

Peace be within thy walls, and prosperity within thy palaces.

Tehillim- Book of Psalms

For my brethren and companions' sakes, I will now say: 'Peace be within thee.'
For the sake of the house of the LORD our God I will seek thy good.

Chapter 123

A Song of Ascents. Unto Thee I lift up mine eyes, O Thou that art enthroned in the heavens.
Behold, as the eyes of servants unto the hand of their master, As the eyes of a maiden unto the hand of her mistress; So our eyes look unto the LORD our God, Until He be gracious unto us.
Be gracious unto us, O LORD, be gracious unto us; For we are full sated with contempt.
Our soul is full sated With the scorning of those that are at ease, And with the contempt of the proud oppressors.

Chapter 124

A Song of Ascents; of David. 'If it had not been the LORD who was for us', Let Israel now say;
'If it had not been the LORD who was for us, When men rose up against us,
Then they had swallowed us up alive, when their wrath was kindled against us;
Then the waters had overwhelmed us, the stream had gone over our soul;
Then the proud waters Had gone over our soul.'

Tehillim- Book of Psalms

Blessed be the LORD, who hath not given us as a prey to their teeth.

Our soul is escaped as a bird out of the snare of the fowlers; The snare is broken, and we are escaped.

Our help is in the name of the LORD, Who made heaven and earth.

Chapter 125

A Song of Ascents. They that trust in the LORD Are as mount Zion, which cannot be moved, but abideth for ever.

As the mountains are round about Jerusalem, So the LORD is round about His people, From this time forth and for ever.

For the rod of wickedness shall not rest upon the lot of the righteous; That the righteous put not forth their hands unto iniquity.

Do good, O LORD, unto the good, And to them that are upright in their hearts.

But as for such as turn aside unto their crooked ways, The LORD will lead them away with the workers of iniquity. Peace be upon Israel.

Chapter 126

A Song of Ascents. When the LORD brought back those that returned to Zion, We were like unto them that dream.

Tehillim- Book of Psalms

Then was our mouth filled with laughter, and our tongue with singing; then said they among the nations: 'The LORD hath done great things with these.'

The LORD hath done great things with us; we are rejoiced.

Turn our captivity, O LORD, as the streams in the dry land.

They that sow in tears Shall reap in joy.

Though he goeth on his way weeping that beareth the measure of seed, He shall come home with joy, bearing his sheaves.

Chapter 127

A Song of Ascents; of Solomon. Except the LORD build the house, They labour in vain that build it; Except the LORD keep the city, The watchman waketh but in vain.

It is vain for you that ye rise early, and sit up late, Ye that eat the bread of toil; So He giveth unto His beloved in sleep.

Lo, children are a heritage of the LORD; The fruit of the womb is a reward.

As arrows in the hand of a mighty man, So are the children of one's youth.

Happy is the man that hath his quiver full of them; They shall not be put to shame, When they speak with their enemies in the gate.

Tehillim- Book of Psalms

Chapter 128

A Song of Ascents. Happy is every one that feareth the LORD, That walketh in His ways.

When thou eatest the labour of thy hands, Happy shalt thou be, and it shall be well with thee.

Thy wife shall be as a fruitful vine, in the innermost parts of thy house; Thy children like olive plants, round about thy table.

Behold, surely thus shall the man be blessed That feareth the LORD.

The LORD bless thee out of Zion; And see thou the good of Jerusalem all the days of thy life;

And see thy children's children. Peace be upon Israel!

Chapter 129

A Song of Ascents. 'Much have they afflicted me from my youth up', Let Israel now say;

'Much have they afflicted me from my youth up; But they have not prevailed against me.

The plowers plowed upon my back; They made long their furrows.

The LORD is righteous; He hath cut asunder the cords of the wicked.'

Let them be ashamed and turned backward, All they that hate Zion.

Let them be as the grass upon the housetops, Which withereth afore it springeth up;

Tehillim- Book of Psalms

Wherewith the reaper filleth not his hand, Nor he that bindeth sheaves his bosom.

Neither do they that go by say: 'The blessing of the LORD be upon you; We bless you in the name of the LORD.'

Chapter 130

A Song of Ascents. Out of the depths have I called Thee, O LORD.

Lord, hearken unto my voice; let Thine ears be attentive to the voice of my supplications.

If Thou, LORD, shouldest mark iniquities, O Lord, who could stand?

For with Thee there is forgiveness, that Thou mayest be feared.

I wait for the LORD, my soul doth wait, and in His word do I hope.

My soul waiteth for the Lord, more than watchmen for the morning; yea, more than watchmen for the morning.

O Israel, hope in the LORD; for with the LORD there is mercy, and with Him is plenteous redemption.

And He will redeem Israel from all his iniquities.

Chapter 131

A Song of Ascents; of David. LORD, my heart is not haughty, nor mine eyes lofty; Neither do I exercise

Tehillim- Book of Psalms

myself in things too great, or in things too wonderful for me.

Surely, I have stilled and quieted my soul; Like a weaned child with his mother; My soul is with me like a weaned child.

O Israel, hope in the LORD From this time forth and for ever.

Chapter 132

A Song of Ascents. LORD, remember unto David All his affliction;

How he swore unto the LORD, And vowed unto the Mighty One of Jacob:

Surely, I will not come into the tent of my house, Nor go up into the bed that is spread for me;

I will not give sleep to mine eyes, Nor slumber to mine eyelids;

Until I find out a place for the LORD, A dwelling-place for the Mighty One of Jacob.'

Lo, we heard of it as being in Ephrath; We found it in the field of athe wood.

Let us go into His dwelling-place; Let us worship at His footstool.

Arise, O LORD, unto Thy resting-place; Thou, and the ark of Thy strength.

Let Thy priests be clothed with righteousness; And let Thy saints shout for joy.

Tehillim- Book of Psalms

For Thy servant David's sake Turn not away the face of Thine anointed.

The LORD swore unto David in truth; He will not turn back from it: 'Of the fruit of thy body will I set upon thy throne.

If thy children keep My covenant And My testimony that I shall teach them, Their children also for ever shall sit upon thy throne.'

For the LORD hath chosen Zion; He hath desired it for His habitation:

'This is My resting-place for ever; Here will I dwell; for I have desired it.

I will abundantly bless her provision; I will give her needy bread in plenty.

Her priests also will I clothe with salvation; And her saints shall shout aloud for joy.

There will I make a horn to shoot up unto David, There have I ordered a lamp for Mine anointed.

His enemies will I clothe with shame; But upon himself shall his crown shine.'

Chapter 133

A Song of Ascents; of David. Behold, how good and how pleasant it is For brethren to dwell together in unity!

It is like the precious oil upon the head, Coming down upon the beard; Even Aaron's beard, That cometh down upon the collar of his garments;

Tehillim- Book of Psalms

Like the dew of Hermon, That cometh down upon the mountains of Zion; For there the LORD commanded the blessing, Even life for ever.

Chapter 134

A Song of Ascents. Behold, bless ye the LORD, all ye servants of the LORD, That stand in the house of the LORD in the night seasons.

Lift up your hands to the sanctuary, And bless ye the LORD.

The LORD bless thee out of Zion; Even He that made heaven and earth.

Chapter 135

Hallelujah. Praise ye the name of the LORD; Give praise, O ye servants of the LORD,

Ye that stand in the house of the LORD, In the courts of the house of our God.

Praise ye the LORD, for the LORD is good; Sing praises unto His name, for it is pleasant.

For the LORD hath chosen Jacob unto Himself, And Israel for His own treasure.

For I know that the LORD is great, And that our Lord is above all gods.

Whatsoever the LORD pleased, that hath He done, In heaven and in earth, in the seas and in all deeps;

Who causeth the vapours to ascend from the ends of the

Tehillim- Book of Psalms

earth; He maketh lightnings for the rain; He bringeth forth the wind out of His treasuries.

Who smote the first-born of Egypt, Both of man and beast.

He sent signs and wonders into the midst of thee, O Egypt, Upon Pharaoh, and upon all his servants.

Who smote many nations, And slew mighty kings:

Sihon king of the Amorites, And Og king of Bashan, And all the kingdoms of Canaan;

And gave their land for a heritage, A heritage unto Israel His people.

O LORD, Thy name endureth for ever; Thy memorial, O LORD, throughout all generations.

For the LORD will judge His people, And repent Himself for His servants.

The idols of the nations are silver and gold, The work of men's hands.

They have mouths, but they speak not; Eyes have they, but they see not;

They have ears, but they hear not; Neither is there any breath in their mouths.

They that make them shall be like unto them; Yea, every one that trusteth in them.

O house of Israel, bless ye the LORD; O house of Aaron, bless ye the LORD;

O house of Levi, bless ye the LORD; Ye that fear the LORD, bless ye the LORD.

Tehillim- Book of Psalms

Blessed be the LORD out of Zion, Who dwelleth at Jerusalem. Hallelujah.

Chapter 136

O give thanks unto the LORD, for He is good, For His mercy endureth for ever.
O give thanks unto the God of gods, For His mercy endureth for ever.
O give thanks unto the Lord of lords, For His mercy endureth for ever.
To Him who alone doeth great wonders, For His mercy endureth for ever.
To Him that by understanding made the heavens, for His mercy endureth for ever.
To Him that spread forth the earth above the waters, For His mercy endureth for ever.
To Him that made great lights, For His mercy endureth for ever;
The sun to rule by day, For His mercy endureth for ever;
The moon and stars to rule by night, For His mercy endureth for ever.
To Him that smote Egypt in their first-born, For His mercy endureth for ever;
And brought out Israel from among them, For His mercy endureth for ever;
With a strong hand, and with an outstretched arm, For His mercy endureth for ever.

Tehillim- Book of Psalms

To Him who divided the Red Sea in sunder, For His mercy endureth for ever;
And made Israel to pass through the midst of it, For His mercy endureth for ever;
But overthrew Pharaoh and his host in the Red Sea, For His mercy endureth for ever.
To Him that led His people through the wilderness, For His mercy endureth for ever.
To Him that smote great kings; For His mercy endureth for ever;
And slew mighty kings, For His mercy endureth for ever.
Sihon king of the Amorites, For His mercy endureth for ever;
And Og king of Bashan, For His mercy endureth for ever;
And gave their land for a heritage, For His mercy endureth for ever;
Even a heritage unto Israel His servant, For His mercy endureth for ever.
Who remembered us in our low estate, For His mercy endureth for ever;
And hath delivered us from our adversaries, For His mercy endureth for ever.
Who giveth food to all flesh, For His mercy endureth for ever.
O give thanks unto the God of heaven, For His mercy endureth for ever.

Tehillim- Book of Psalms

Chapter 137

By the rivers of Babylon, There we sat down, yea, we wept, When we remembered Zion.

Upon the willows in the midst thereof We hanged up our harps.

For there they that led us captive asked of us words of song, And our tormentors asked of us mirth: 'Sing us one of the songs of Zion.'

How shall we sing the LORD'S song In a foreign land?

If I forget thee, O Jerusalem, Let my right hand forget her cunning.

Let my tongue cleave to the roof of my mouth, If I remember thee not; If I set not Jerusalem Above my chiefest joy.

Remember, O LORD, against the children of Edom The day of Jerusalem; Who said: 'Rase it, rase it, Even to the foundation thereof.'

O daughter of Babylon, that art to be destroyed; Happy shall he be, that repayeth thee As thou hast served us.

Happy shall he be, that taketh and dasheth thy little ones Against the rock.

Chapter 138

A Psalm of David. I will give Thee thanks with my whole heart, In the presence of the mighty will I sing praises unto Thee.

I will bow down toward Thy holy temple, And give

Tehillim- Book of Psalms

thanks unto Thy name for Thy mercy and for Thy truth; For Thou hast magnified Thy word above all Thy name.

In the day that I called, Thou didst answer me; Thou didst encourage me in my soul with strength.

All the kings of the earth shall give Thee thanks, O LORD, For they have heard the words of Thy mouth.

Yea, they shall sing of the ways of the LORD; For great is the glory of the LORD.

For though the LORD be high, yet regardeth He the lowly, And the haughty He knoweth from afar.

Though I walk in the midst of trouble, Thou quickenest me; Thou stretchest forth Thy hand against the wrath of mine enemies, And Thy right hand doth save me.

The LORD will accomplish that which concerneth me; Thy mercy, O LORD, endureth for ever; Forsake not the work of Thine own hands.

Chapter 139

For the Leader. A Psalm of David. O LORD, Thou hast searched me, and known me.

Thou knowest my downsitting and mine uprising, Thou understandest my thought afar off.

Thou measurest my going about and my lying down, And art acquainted with all my ways.

For there is not a word in my tongue, But, lo, O LORD, Thou knowest it altogether.

Thou hast hemmed me in behind and before, And laid

Tehillim- Book of Psalms

Thy hand upon me.

Such knowledge is too wonderful for me; Too high, I cannot attain unto it.

Whither shall I go from Thy spirit? Or whither shall I flee from Thy presence?

If I ascend up into heaven, Thou art there; If I make my bed in the nether-world, behold, Thou art there.

If I take the wings of the morning, And dwell in the uttermost parts of the sea;

Even there would Thy hand lead me, And Thy right hand would hold me.

And if I say: 'Surely the darkness shall envelop me, And the light about me shall be night';

Even the darkness is not too dark for Thee, But the night shineth as the day; The darkness is even as the light.

For Thou hast made my reins; Thou hast knit me together in my mother's womb.

I will give thanks unto Thee, for I am fearfully and wonderfully made; Wonderful are Thy works; and that my soul knoweth right well.

My frame was not hidden from Thee, When I was made in secret, And curiously wrought in the lowest parts of the earth.

Thine eyes did see mine unformed substance, And in Thy book they were all written— Even the days that were fashioned, When as yet there was none of them.

How weighty also are Thy thoughts unto me, O God!

Tehillim- Book of Psalms

How great is the sum of them!
If I would count them, they are more in number than the sand; Were I to come to the end of them, I would still be with Thee.
If Thou but wouldest slay the wicked, O God— Depart from me therefore, ye men of blood;
Who utter Thy name with wicked thought, They take it for falsehood, even Thine enemies—.
Do not I hate them, O LORD, that hate Thee? And do not I strive with those that rise up against Thee?
I hate them with utmost hatred; I count them mine enemies.
Search me, O God, and know my heart, Try me, and know my thoughts;
And see if there be any way in me that is grievous, And lead me in the way everlasting.

Chapter 140
For the Leader. A Psalm of David.
Deliver me, O LORD, from the evil man; Preserve me from the violent man;
Who devise evil things in their heart; Every day do they stir up wars.
They have sharpened their tongue like a serpent; Vipers' venom is under their lips. Selah
Keep me, O LORD, from the hands of the wicked; Preserve me from the violent man; Who have purposed

Tehillim- Book of Psalms

to make my steps slip.

The proud have hid a snare for me, and cords; They have spread a net by the wayside; They have set gins for me. Selah

I have said unto the LORD: 'Thou art my God'; Give ear, O LORD, unto the voice of my supplications.

O GOD the Lord, the strength of my salvation, Who hast screened my head in the day of battle,

Grant not, O LORD, the desires of the wicked; Further not his evil device, so that they exalt themselves. Selah

As for the head of those that compass me about, Let the mischief of their own lips cover them.

Let burning coals fall upon them; Let them be cast into the fire, into deep pits, that they rise not up again.

A slanderer shall not be established in the earth; The violent and evil man shall be hunted with thrust upon thrust.

I know that the LORD will maintain the cause of the poor, And the right of the needy.

Surely the righteous shall give thanks unto Thy name; The upright shall dwell in Thy presence.

Chapter 141

A Psalm of David. LORD, I have called Thee; make haste unto me; Give ear unto my voice, when I call unto Thee. Let my prayer be set forth as incense before Thee, The lifting up of my hands as the evening sacrifice.

Tehillim- Book of Psalms

Set a guard, O LORD, to my mouth; Keep watch at the door of my lips.

Incline not my heart to any evil thing, To be occupied in deeds of wickedness With men that work iniquity; And let me not eat of their dainties.

Let the righteous smite me in kindness, and correct me; Oil so choice let not my head refuse; For still is my prayer because of their wickedness.

Their judges are thrown down by the sides of the rock; And they shall hear my words, that they are sweet.

As when one cleaveth and breaketh up the earth, Our bones are scattered at the grave's mouth.

For mine eyes are unto Thee, O GOD the Lord; In Thee have I taken refuge, O pour not out my soul.

Keep me from the snare which they have laid for me, And from the gins of the workers of iniquity.

Let the wicked fall into their own nets, Whilst I withal escape.

Chapter 142

Maschil of David, when he was in the cave; a Prayer.

With my voice I cry unto the LORD; With my voice I make supplication unto the LORD.

I pour out my complaint before Him, I declare before Him my trouble;

When my spirit fainteth within me - Thou knowest my path – In the way wherein I walk Have they hidden a

Tehillim- Book of Psalms

snare for me.

Look on my right hand, and see, For there is no man that knoweth me; I have no way to flee; No man careth for my soul.

I have cried unto Thee, O LORD; I have said: 'Thou art my refuge, My portion in the land of the living.'

Attend unto my cry; For I am brought very low; Deliver me from my persecutors; For they are too strong for me.

Bring my soul out of prison, That I may give thanks unto Thy name; The righteous shall crown themselves because of me; For Thou wilt deal bountifully with me.

Chapter 143

A Psalm of David. O LORD, hear my prayer, give ear to my supplications; In Thy faithfulness answer me, and in Thy righteousness.

And enter not into judgment with Thy servant; For in Thy sight shall no man living be justified.

For the enemy hath persecuted my soul; He hath crushed my life down to the ground; He hath made me to dwell in darkness, as those that have been long dead.

And my spirit fainteth within me; My heart within me is appalled.

I remember the days of old; I meditate on all Thy doing; I muse on the work of Thy hands.

I spread forth my hands unto Thee; My soul thirsteth after Thee, as a weary land. Selah

Tehillim- Book of Psalms

Answer me speedily, O LORD, My spirit faileth; Hide not Thy face from me; Lest I become like them that go down into the pit.
Cause me to hear Thy lovingkindness in the morning, For in Thee do I trust; Cause me to know the way wherein I should walk, For unto Thee have I lifted up my soul.
Deliver me from mine enemies, O LORD; With Thee have I hidden myself.
Teach me to do Thy will, For Thou art my God; Let Thy good spirit Lead me in an even land.
For Thy name's sake, O LORD, quicken me; In Thy righteousness bring my soul out of trouble.
And in Thy mercy cut off mine enemies, And destroy all them that harass my soul; For I am Thy servant.

Chapter 144
A Psalm of David. Blessed be the LORD my Rock, Who traineth my hands for war, And my fingers for battle;
My lovingkindness, and my fortress, My high tower, and my deliverer; My shield, and He in whom I take refuge; Who subdueth my people under me.
LORD, what is man, that Thou takest knowledge of him? Or the son of man, that Thou makest account of him?
Man is like unto a breath; His days are as a shadow that passeth away.
O LORD, bow Thy heavens, and come down; Touch the mountains, that they may smoke.

Tehillim- Book of Psalms

Cast forth lightning, and scatter them; Send out Thine arrows, and discomfit them.

Stretch forth Thy hands from on high; Rescue me, and deliver me out of many waters, Out of the hand of strangers;

Whose mouth speaketh falsehood, And their right hand is a right hand of lying.

O God, I will sing a new song unto Thee, Upon a psaltery of ten strings will I sing praises unto Thee;

Who givest salvation unto kings, Who rescuest David Thy servant from the hurtful sword.

Rescue me, and deliver me out of the hand of strangers, Whose mouth speaketh falsehood, And their right hand is a right hand of lying.

We whose sons are as plants grown up in their youth; Whose daughters are as corner-pillars carved after the fashion of a palace;

Whose garners are full, affording all manner of store; Whose sheep increase by thousands and ten thousands in our fields;

Whose oxen are well laden; With no breach, and no going forth, And no outcry in our broad places;

Happy is the people that is in such a case. Yea, happy is the people whose God is the LORD.

Chapter 145

A Psalm of praise; of David. I will extol Thee, my God,

Tehillim- Book of Psalms

O King; And I will bless Thy name for ever and ever.
Every day will I bless Thee; And I will praise Thy name for ever and ever.
Great is the LORD, and highly to be praised; And His greatness is unsearchable.
One generation shall laud Thy works to another, And shall declare Thy mighty acts.
The glorious splendour of Thy majesty, And Thy wondrous works, will I rehearse.
And men shall speak of the might of Thy tremendous acts; And I will tell of Thy greatness.
They shall utter the fame of Thy great goodness, And shall sing of Thy righteousness.
The LORD is gracious, and full of compassion; Slow to anger, and of great mercy.
The LORD is good to all; And His tender mercies are over all His works.
All Thy works shall praise Thee, O LORD; And Thy saints shall bless Thee.
They shall speak of the glory of Thy kingdom, And talk of Thy might;
To make known to the sons of men His mighty acts, And the glory of the majesty of His kingdom.
Thy kingdom is a kingdom for all ages, And Thy dominion endureth throughout all generations.
The LORD upholdeth all that fall, And raiseth up all those that are bowed down.

Tehillim- Book of Psalms

The eyes of all wait for Thee, And Thou givest them their food in due season.

Thou openest Thy hand, And satisfiest every living thing with favour.

The LORD is righteous in all His ways, And gracious in all His works.

The LORD is nigh unto all them that call upon Him, To all that call upon Him in truth.

He will fulfil the desire of them that fear Him; He also will hear their cry, and will save them.

The LORD preserveth all them that love Him; But all the wicked will He destroy.

My mouth shall speak the praise of the LORD; And let all flesh bless His holy name for ever and ever.

Chapter 146

Hallelujah. Praise the LORD, O my soul.

I will praise the LORD while I live; I will sing praises unto my God while I have my being.

Put not your trust in princes, Nor in the son of man, in whom there is no help.

His breath goeth forth, he returneth to his dust; In that very day his thoughts perish.

Happy is he whose help is the God of Jacob, Whose hope is in the LORD his God,

Who made heaven and earth, The sea, and all that in them is; Who keepeth truth for ever;

Tehillim- Book of Psalms

Who executeth justice for the oppressed; Who giveth bread to the hungry. The LORD looseth the prisoners;

The LORD openeth the eyes of the blind; The LORD raiseth up them that are bowed down; The LORD loveth the righteous;

The LORD preserveth the strangers; He upholdeth the fatherless and the widow; But the way of the wicked He maketh crooked.

The LORD will reign for ever, Thy God, O Zion, unto all generations. Hallelujah.

Chapter 147

Hallelujah; For it is good to sing praises unto our God; For it is pleasant, and praise is comely.

The LORD doth build up Jerusalem, He gathereth together the dispersed of Israel;

Who healeth the broken in heart, And bindeth up their wounds.

He counteth the number of the stars; He giveth them all their names.

Great is our Lord, and mighty in power; His understanding is infinite.

The LORD upholdeth the humble; He bringeth the wicked down to the ground.

Sing unto the LORD with thanksgiving, Sing praises upon the harp unto our God;

Who covereth the heaven with clouds, Who prepareth

Tehillim- Book of Psalms

rain for the earth, Who maketh the mountains to spring with grass.

He giveth to the beast his food, And to the young ravens which cry.

He delighteth not in the strength of the horse; He taketh no pleasure in the legs of a man.

The LORD taketh pleasure in them that fear Him, In those that wait for His mercy.

Glorify the LORD, O Jerusalem; Praise thy God, O Zion.

For He hath made strong the bars of thy gates; He hath blessed thy children within thee.

He maketh thy borders peace; He giveth thee in plenty the fat of wheat.

He sendeth out His commandment upon earth; His word runneth very swiftly.

He giveth snow like wool; He scattereth the hoar-frost like ashes.

He casteth forth His ice like crumbs; Who can stand before His cold?

He sendeth forth His word, and melteth them; He causeth His wind to blow, and the waters flow.

He declareth His word unto Jacob, His statutes and His ordinances unto Israel.

He hath not dealt so with any nation; And as for His ordinances, they have not known them. Hallelujah.

Tehillim- Book of Psalms

Chapter 148

Hallelujah. Praise ye the LORD from the heavens; Praise Him in the heights.

Praise ye Him, all His angels; Praise ye Him, all His hosts.

Praise ye Him, sun and moon; Praise Him, all ye stars of light.

Praise Him, ye heavens of heavens, And ye waters that are above the heavens.

Let them praise the name of the LORD; For He commanded, and they were created.

He hath also established them for ever and ever; He hath made a decree which shall not be transgressed.

Praise the LORD from the earth, Ye sea-monsters, and all deeps;

Fire and hail, snow and vapour, Stormy wind, fulfilling His word;

Mountains and all hills, Fruitful trees and all cedars;

Beasts and all cattle, Creeping things and winged fowl;

Kings of the earth and all peoples, Princes and all judges of the earth;

Both young men and maidens, Old men and children;

Let them praise the name of the LORD, For His name alone is exalted; His glory is above the earth and heaven.

And He hath lifted up a horn for His people, A praise for all His saints, Even for the children of Israel, a people near unto Him. Hallelujah.

Tehillim- Book of Psalms

Chapter 149

Hallelujah. Sing unto the LORD a new song, And His praise in the assembly of the saints.

Let Israel rejoice in his Maker; Let the children of Zion be joyful in their King.

Let them praise His name in the dance; Let them sing praises unto Him with the timbrel and harp.

For the LORD taketh pleasure in His people; He adorneth the humble with salvation.

Let the saints exult in glory; Let them sing for joy upon their beds.

Let the high praises of God be in their mouth, And a two-edged sword in their hand;

To execute vengeance upon the nations, And chastisements upon the peoples;

To bind their kings with chains, And their nobles with fetters of iron;

To execute upon them the judgment written; He is the glory of all His saints. Hallelujah.

Chapter 150

He is the glory of all His saints.

Praise Him for His mighty acts; Praise Him according to His abundant greatness.

Praise Him with the blast of the horn; Praise Him with the psaltery and harp.

Praise Him with the timbrel and dance; Praise Him with

Tehillim- Book of Psalms

stringed instruments and the pipe.

Praise Him with the loud-sounding cymbals; Praise Him with the clanging cymbals.

Let every thing that hath breath praise the LORD. Hallelujah.

Tehillim- Book of Psalms

www.ingramcontent.com/pod-product-compliance
Lightning Source LLC
Chambersburg PA
CBHW070136080526
44586CB00015B/1714